the Flirtation Experiment WORKBOOK

30 ACTS TO ADDING MAGIC, MYSTERY, AND SPARK TO YOUR EVERYDAY MARRIAGE

Workbook | Six Sessions

LISA JACOBSON and
PHYLICIA MASONHEIMER

The Flirtation Experiment Workbook

Requests for information should be addressed to:
HarperChristian Resources, 3900 Sparks Dr. SE, Grand Rapids, Michigan 49546

ISBN 978–0–310–14097–9 (softcover)

ISBN 978–0–310–14098–6 (ebook)

HarperChristian Resources titles may be purchased in bulk for church, business, fundraising, or ministry use. For information, please e-mail ResourceSpecialist@ChurchSource.com.

The author is represented by Alive Literary Agency, www.aliveliterary.com.

First Printing September 2021 / Printed in the United States of America

Contents

Before We Begin

Preface and Introduction

Welcome to the Flirtation Experiment.

We are so grateful that you are here! Whatever you might be feeling and thinking right now, just know that you are so welcome on this journey with us. The Flirtation Experiment changed and challenged our marriages in ways that we didn't know were possible, but we're so grateful that we gave it a chance.

We're hoping that this workbook will help you record your thoughts throughout the experiment. Use the sections that help you and challenge you. Some sections are meant to help you plan out your experiments, others are meant to help you recollect on them. If anything feels like extra work, leave it out!

Let's start off with a question: About spark, mystery, romance, and flirting, Phylicia asks in the preface, "Why do so many of these things end when people get married?"

Why do those things end when we get married? Have they ended or changed for you?

What do you think?

Before We Begin

PRE-EXPERIMENT QUESTIONS

Welcome to the Flirtation Experiment! Let's answer a few more questions, complete an overview of your marriage, and then discuss the setup of the workbook.

1. In a Christian marriage, who is the "pursuer"?

2. Read these verses from the Song of Solomon:

> "Come, my beloved,
> Let us go forth to the field;
> Let us lodge in the villages.
> Let us get up early to the vineyards;
> Let us see if the vine has budded,
> Whether the grape blossoms are open,
> And the pomegranates are in bloom.
> There I will give you my love.
> The mandrakes give off a fragrance,
> And at our gates are pleasant fruits,
> All manner, new and old,
> Which I have laid up for you, my beloved" (Song of Solomon 7:11–13 NKJV)

Who is speaking? King Solomon, or his lover?

3. Grab a Bible and look up Song of Solomon 7:10. Cast yourself in the role of the speaker–what would it be like to say those things to your husband?

4. What were you taught about flirtation as a teenager? Do you remember specific conversations with your parents, friends, or pastors about the topic?

5. What are your initial feelings about the idea of flirting more with your husband? Circle where you think you're at on the line chart below–even if you're in two or three places at once!–and then write about why you think you feel that way.

Terrified Anxious Cautious Curious Eager Thrilled

6. Would you say that you already flirt with your husband? That he flirts with you? Do you believe that your marriage might benefit from even more of these kinds of playful interactions?

7. What are your expectations about flirting more with your husband? What are you hoping for–what's the best thing that could happen? Do you think he'll be quick to respond to your efforts or slow to respond to them?

MARRIAGE OVERVIEW

1. How long have you been married? When is your anniversary?

2. Do you have any children? How old are they, and what are their names?

3. Who works where? We've both been at home with our kids, and we know that it's hard work! If one of you is staying at home with children, include that when you're discussing work!

4. Is there anything else that you think is pertinent to include about your marriage, especially if you're doing this study with a group?

WORKBOOK SETUP

The goal of the workbook is to help you customize the Flirtation Experiment to your marriage. Read through the table of contents. Which experiment titles stick out to you?

The workbook has six sessions, and each session is made up of five separate experiments. The workbook follows the same order as *The Flirtation Experiment* book. The workbook space dedicated to each experiment has a recap of the chapter, a spot for brainstorming your own experiment, and some wrap-up questions that will help you reflect on how your experiment went.

A brief note about the visual tracker below–some women find tools like this tracker helpful. Others might feel more neutral about using a tool like this. And for some women, sticking a number down on a line to describe their marriages will feel like nothing but failure tracker. If this is you . . . don't use this tool! Find another way to describe your thoughts, feelings, and process throughout the Flirtation Experiment.

At the end of each session, you'll find the following visual tracker:

On these scales, one is "Never," five is "Sometimes" and ten is "Always."

Intentional: I take specific actions to strengthen our marriage and show him that I love him.

Never				Sometimes					Always
1	2	3	4	5	6	7	8	9	10

Faithful: I am a safe place for him. I do not mock him or call him names. He can tell me things and be confident that I won't tell everyone else.

Never				Sometimes					Always
1	2	3	4	5	6	7	8	9	10

Hopeful: I am grateful for our past and I see redemption in it, even in the difficult things. I am excited about our future together.

Never				Sometimes					Always
1	2	3	4	5	6	7	8	9	10

Joyful: We do more together than just the necessities—we create time for each other and we laugh together.

Never Sometimes Always

1	2	3	4	5	6	7	8	9	10

Covenantal: I am confident that, through God's grace, we will uphold our marriage covenant.

Never Sometimes Always

1	2	3	4	5	6	7	8	9	10

Go ahead and fill in the tracker for where you think your marriage is at right now—you can check back in with it as you progress through the experiments.

At the end of the book, you'll find an appendix with questions for your husband. Check out the appendix for more information about how to use it.

Let's get started!

Session One

Love Rejoices

Affection, Passion, Playfulness, Kindness, Desire

Chapters 1 – 5

Okay. Are you ready to start your own experiments?

You're probably feeling a little nervous, but hopefully you're feeling some excitement, too. In some ways, though, it doesn't matter if you *feel* ready or not! You can still start somewhere. You don't want the romance to be over just because you've been married for a year–or for ten–or for twenty or more! Start rejoicing in the gift of marriage with the first five flirtation experiments–experiments of affection, passion, playfulness, kindness, and desire.

Maybe you've never been the initiator of romance in your relationship, and you're feeling intimidated by a new role. Maybe you're afraid that no matter how creative you are, you won't get any response from him. No matter what fears or hesitations you are dealing with, God knows your heart. He knows your desire for more joy in your marriage.

Ask for His help. Some of the steps you take may feel awkward or halting, and there will certainly be disappointments and unmet expectations. But joy in your marriage is worth the awkwardness–and even the total failures!

Consider this an invitation to rejoice in the gift of your marriage–even if it feels strange at first.

Chapter 1

RECAP: AFFECTION

Phylicia knew that her husband Josh felt loved when she touched him. She wanted to show him love in a way he understood, even if she didn't understand the need for touch very well herself. Before she started her experiment, she realized that her fear of rejection made her keep her distance from Josh. What if she touched him and he didn't respond? Phylicia's first flirtation experiment helped her push past this fear. She gave Josh nonsexual, affirming touches throughout a regular day. Josh responded to her efforts with grace and gratitude–even though her efforts felt awkward. Both of them felt loved by giving and receiving simple, affectionate touches.

"Those first couple times expressing affectionate touch felt completely antithetical to my personality. This made me nervous because I didn't want to feel like I was faking something. I wanted my actions to be genuine." (From *The Flirtation Experiment*, page 4)

Can you relate to Phylicia's thoughts? Do you enjoy touching other people, or does affection through touch feel disingenuous or even uncomfortable to you?

____

____

____

____

"For you did not receive the spirit of bondage again to fear, but you received the Spirit of adoption by whom we cry out, "Abba, Father." (Romans 8:15 NKJV)

Father God, you broke through every barrier to show me affection, and to give me the spirit of adoption instead of the spirit of fear. If there is something that is holding me back from my husband, please show it to me. Help me take a small step to foster affection in my marriage.

MY {AFFECTION} EXPERIMENT

Brainstorming: Touch him without any agenda–touch him just to tell him that you are there and that you care about him. Touch his shoulder. Sit next to him instead of across from him. Squeeze his arm. Try a kiss before you part for the day instead of a wave. Offer him your hand when you're close by.

My Plan: Pick ONE specific action for your {Affection} experiment.

WHAT I'm going to do:

WHEN I'm going to do it:

Anything I need to prepare in advance:

My {Affection} Experiment Reflection:

What Happened:

List a few things about your {Affection} Experiment that . . .

Encouraged You:	*Disappointed you:*	*Surprised you:*

Our Obstacles:

His Response:

MY {AFFECTION} EXPERIMENT WRAP-UP

To Ponder: Are you afraid that your husband will reject you–not just your affectionate touches, but you as a person? What could be the underlying cause of that fear?

More {Affection}: Phylicia quotes the C.S. Lewis book, *The Four Loves*. Lewis writes, "Lock it up safe in the casket. . . . [and] it will become unbreakable, impenetrable, irredeemable."* The possibility of showing affection begins with being vulnerable, with "unlocking." Do you feel the need for "unlocking" in your life; in the union you share with your husband?

Preparing For Your Next Experiment: Can you remember a time that you shrugged your husband off, maybe when he was trying to give you attention or affection?

Chapter 2

RECAP: PASSION

Lisa remembers a time that she initially shrugged off her husband Matt, but then changed the moment by giving him a passionate response. At this time in her life, Lisa and Matt had several young kids, and Lisa felt very busy and frazzled. She thought that passion was going to have to wait for a different season of their marriage. But leaning into Matt changed things for both of them; Lisa's choice made room for passion in the middle of the craziness of an ordinary day.

*C. S. Lewis, "Charity," *The Four Loves* (New York: HarperCollins, 2017), 155–156.

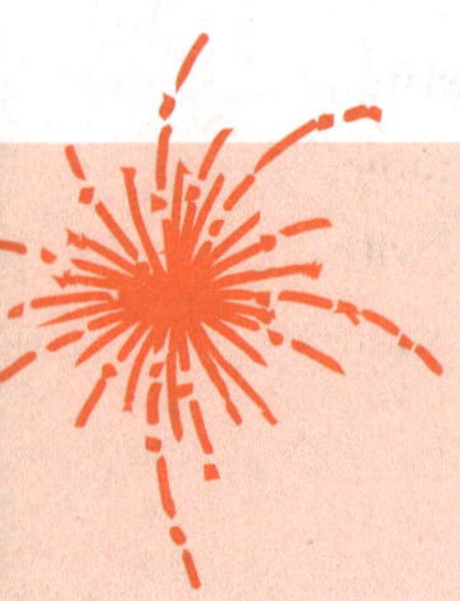

"Now, you may be asking yourself what place passion has in a Christian marriage. Isn't that a rather worldly, self-focused pursuit? A way of thinking better suited for chick flicks and romance novels? Something you leave behind not long after the honeymoon?" (From *The Flirtation Experiment*, page 9)

Where did you last see or hear the word "passion;" maybe in a movie, or a novel, or an advertisement? Do you associate the word "passion" with marriage? Do you think of passion as a selfish pursuit, an opportunity for self-giving, or something in between?

"I am my beloved's,
And his desire is toward me.
Come, my beloved,
Let us go forth to the field;
Let us lodge in the villages.
Let us get up early to the vineyards;
Let us see if the vine has budded,
Whether the grape blossoms are open,
And the pomegranates are in bloom.
There I will give you my love." (Song of Solomon 7:10–12 NKJV)

Lord, You designed marriage for passion, throughout every season, not just the newlywed and empty nester phases. Help me to say to my husband, "Come, my beloved," even if it's difficult.

MY {PASSION} EXPERIMENT

Brainstorming: Move toward your husband with the intention of making him feel wanted and welcomed. Respond generously when he reaches out to you, especially if you're in the middle of doing something else. When you first see each other at the end of a long day, move toward him before you do anything else. Linger at the end of a kiss instead of pulling away. Reach out to him–sensually, even!

My Plan: Pick ONE specific action for your {Passion} experiment.

WHAT I'm going to do:

WHEN I'm going to do it:

Anything I need to prepare in advance:

What Happened:

List a few things about your {Passion} Experiment that . . .

Encouraged You:	*Disappointed you:*	*Surprised you:*

Our Obstacles:

___

___

___

His Response:

___

___

___

MY {PASSION} EXPERIMENT WRAP-UP

To Ponder: Lisa remembers that, right before the passionate moment in the kitchen, she felt "drab–both undesiring and undesirable." Nothing about Lisa's appearance changed. Her *action* led to the change in her feelings. Can you remember a time (it doesn't have to have anything to do with your marriage) when you had to get your actions in order before your feelings would follow?

___

___

___

More {Passion}: Lisa defines passion as "that strong feeling of physical desire and closeness for each other—an intense longing." Do you want to "long" for your husband? Or does that idea create some resistance in you–explore your willingness and/or resistance to the phrase "an intense longing."

___

___

___

Preparing For Your Next Experiment: Does he have any hobbies that you are willing to tolerate, but he loves?

___

___

___

Chapter 3

RECAP: PLAYFULNESS

Phylicia's playfulness experiment required her to do something she never thought she would do: play video games with her husband. She spent the previous days pulling harmless pranks on Josh, which had great results. Then, she felt the Lord calling her to spend time with Josh by playing video games with him, even though she had always hated the games. But she found out that her dislike went deeper than that–any kind of play involves risk, including the risk of looking stupid. Because she didn't want to take that chance, she was holding herself back from intimacy with Josh. To everyone's surprise, she actually enjoyed the time they spent gaming together.

"As time went on, we came to an agreement that Josh would play video games only once or twice a week, usually when the girls were in bed. This seemed fair. 'You do you, bro,' was my attitude on the subject—although my distaste for the games had not lessened." (From *The Flirtation Experiment*, page 14)

Does your husband engage in a hobby or activity that elicits a "You do you, bro" response from you? Imagine doing that activity with your husband. Do you feel comfortable or out of place in the setting of that activity?

"With all humility and gentleness, with patience, bearing with one another in love, eager to maintain the unity of the Spirit in the bond of peace." (Ephesians 4:2–3 ESV)

God, how do you want me to play more in marriage? Please give me the eagerness that Paul writes about in Ephesians. Give me the willingness to risk whatever it is You are asking me to risk.

MY {PLAYFULNESS} EXPERIMENT

Brainstorming: Maybe you need to start with some pranks–introduce a little goofiness to the daily routine! Or, re-create a date you both loved, even if it was something silly like mini-golf or the arcade. Maybe it's time to take a big risk–how does he love to play? Ask if you can play, too.

My Plan: Pick ONE specific action for your {Playfulness} experiment.

WHAT I'm going to do:

WHEN I'm going to do it:

Anything I need to prepare in advance:

My {Playfulness} Experiment Reflection:

What Happened:

List a few things about your {Playfulness} Experiment that . . .

Encouraged You:	*Disappointed you:*	*Surprised you:*

Our Obstacles:

His Response:

MY {PLAYFULNESS} EXPERIMENT WRAP-UP

To Ponder: In the chapter, Phylicia brings up this point: "One reason we avoid play is because of the risk. Being playful exposes us." Do you find ways to play throughout your own day, or do you avoid doing new things and taking risks? In what specific ways does play expose you?

More {Playfulness}: An essential part of good play is a non-judgmental attitude. Have you ever found yourself judging your husband, particularly when he was trying to do something new? Have you ever felt judged by him when you were trying something new? Maybe you feel the most pressure coming from your *own* thoughts! What steps could you take to have a different attitude during playful, risky, or new activities–a different attitude toward *both* yourself and your husband?

Preparing For Your Next Experiment: You've set aside time to meet with a friend. But ten minutes after you meet, she suddenly has to leave due to an unforeseen situation. How do you speak to her as she's leaving?

Chapter 4

RECAP: KINDNESS

Lisa had to choose: she could show kindness to a frustrated and overwhelmed cashier, or she could treat the cashier with disregard. Lisa chose kindness, not knowing that she'd have to make the same decision later that day with someone much closer to her: Matt. Matt called her to cancel an appointment they'd planned a long time ago. Lisa's first inclination was to snap at him over the phone, but she remembered the moment in the grocery store when she'd chosen kindness. She'd chosen to show kindness to a stranger–couldn't she do the same for her husband?

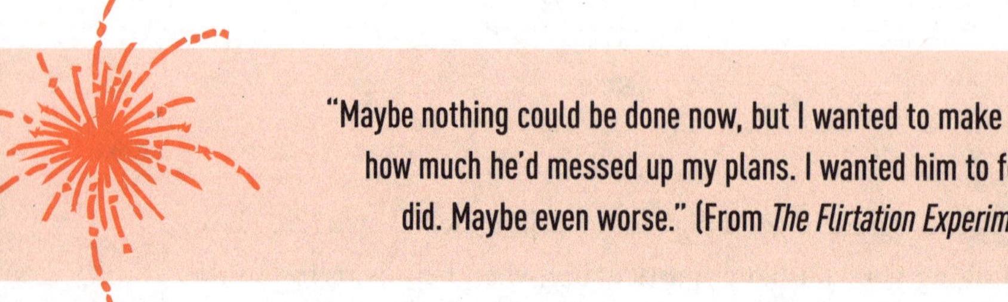

"Maybe nothing could be done now, but I wanted to make sure he understood how much he'd messed up my plans. I wanted him to feel as badly as I did. Maybe even worse." (From *The Flirtation Experiment*, page 21)

If you've ever been vindictive in your interactions with your husband, please know that you are *not* alone. Choosing kindness is a daily battle for each of us. Have you ever felt like Lisa felt–have you ever "wanted him to feel as badly as [you] did"? What does it look like when you act on that feeling?

"Therefore, as God's chosen ones, holy and dearly loved, put on compassion, kindness, humility, gentleness, and patience." (Colossians 3:12 CSB)

Heavenly Father, you call me chosen. In the light of Your great love for me, help me to "put on" kindness. Help me to choose kindness every day, especially in my interactions with my husband.

MY {KINDNESS} EXPERIMENT

Brainstorming: First, think of times throughout the day when you have typically had trouble being kind to your husband. Maybe it's first thing in the morning, maybe it's during the transitions between activities. Maybe you're like Lisa, and it's when he tells you he's going to be late. Then, make the choice ahead of time: *I'm going to choose kind words and kind actions during/when/if* ______________.

My Plan: Pick ONE specific action for your {Kindness} experiment.

WHAT I'm going to do:

WHEN I'm going to do it:

Anything I need to prepare in advance:

MY {KINDNESS} EXPERIMENT REFLECTION:

What Happened:

List a few things about your {Kindness} Experiment that . . .

Encouraged You:	*Disappointed you:*	*Surprised you:*

Our Obstacles:

His Response:

MY {KINDNESS} EXPERIMENT WRAP-UP

To Ponder: Lisa writes, "Somewhere I got this idea that if someone loves you, then you should be 'honest' with them, and they should be able to take it." Can you resonate with Lisa's thoughts here? Do you see this dynamic playing out in your marriage, in either or both directions—do one or both of you come to the table with the attitude, "they should be able to take it"?

More {Kindness}: Actions begin as thoughts—this is true with kind actions, too. It might be useful to become more aware of the thoughts cropping up about your husband. Just for a day, keep a sticky note nearby. When a thought about your husband occurs to you, track it with tally marks—would you categorize that thought as kind or unkind? What did you learn about your thought patterns?

Preparing For Your Next Experiment: When you were single, how often did you assume married couples had sex? What expectations did you have about how often you and your husband would have sex? Has the time you've spent married challenged your assumptions and expectations?

Chapter 5

RECAP: DESIRE

Phylicia had always had more sexual drive than Josh. After being married for a while, her expectations met up with reality. She understood that sex wasn't going to be—and didn't have to be—an every-single-day event. But she also knew that prioritizing some time for sex was very important for both of them. So even during the trying postpartum season,

Phylicia exercised some creativity and created an atmosphere of desire. She wanted to let Josh know that he was wanted.

> **"Josh needed to know I desired him as a person, to be with him in general, not just in the bedroom. He needed to know I liked him, not just loved him, and that I liked him for who he was—not just what he could do for me." (From *The Flirtation Experiment*, page 28)**

Steamy scenes from Hollywood don't tell us anything about real desire. Neither do unbiblical teachings like "you need to have sex, or your husband will stray." To be desired is to be wanted as a *person*, not as a performer going through a series of actions or duties. Do you like your husband for who he is, not just for what he can do for you? Do you believe that he feels the same about you?

> Let your fountain be blessed,
> and take pleasure in the wife of your youth.
> A loving deer, a graceful doe—
> let her breasts always satisfy you;
> be lost in her love forever. (Proverbs 5:18–19 CSB)

Lord God, thank You again for our marriage. I want to be lost in his love forever, and I want him to be lost in mine. We want to rejoice in one another for who we are. Help us to desire one another.

MY {DESIRE} EXPERIMENT

Brainstorming: This experiment is about expressing who you are. What do you love? Do you love beautiful lace and sweet-smelling candles? What about a cozy atmosphere at home, or an afternoon adventure? Maybe even a night on the town at a favorite restaurant?

Chances are, he absolutely loves it when you tell him, "I want to be exactly who I am, and I want you exactly for who you are." Try it!

My Plan: Pick ONE specific action for your {Desire} experiment.

WHAT I'm going to do:

WHEN I'm going to do it:

Anything I need to prepare in advance:

MY {DESIRE} EXPERIMENT REFLECTION:

What Happened:

List a few things about your {Desire} Experiment that . . .

Encouraged You:	*Disappointed you:*	*Surprised you:*

Our Obstacles:

His Response:

MY {DESIRE} EXPERIMENT WRAP-UP

Phylicia writes, "I had no concept of the ups and downs of life together and how that can alter desire through the years." How has your desire for your husband changed throughout the time you have been married?

More {Desire}: There are so many confusing messages out there regarding what the Bible says about sex. Let's look at something it actually does say. This is 1 Corinthians 7:4, ESV: "For the wife does not have authority over her own body, but the husband does. Likewise the husband does not have authority over his own body, but the wife does." This verse highlights the mutual nature of desire in marriage. What do you think it means for him to have authority over your body? For you to have authority over his?

Preparing For Your Next Experiment: What does your daily routine as a couple look like? When was the last time something interrupted that routine–something that was not an errand?

Session One Conclusion:

Love Rejoices

AFFECTION, PASSION, PLAYFULNESS, KINDNESS, DESIRE

You did it–you got started. You pushed past the fear, and you made some definitive choices to start rejoicing–or to rejoice even more deeply–in the gift of your marriage. There were some awkward moments along the way, but rejoicing in your marriage doesn't require you (or your husband) to be perfect in your attempts and responses! Just by stepping out, you've asked God for joy in your marriage.

This tracker uses a scale of one to ten, one being "Never," five being "Sometimes" and ten being "Always." Go with your first instinct, not with what you think you are supposed to say.

NOTE: If this tracker isn't helpful, DON'T USE IT. This is about honest time for reflection–not condemnation or judgment of yourself.

Intentional: I take specific actions to strengthen our marriage and show him that I love him.

Never | Sometimes | Always

1	2	3	4	5	6	7	8	9	10

Faithful: I am a safe place for him. I do not mock him or call him names. He can tell me things and be confident that I won't tell everyone else.

Never | Sometimes | Always

1	2	3	4	5	6	7	8	9	10

Hopeful: I am grateful for our past and I see redemption in it, even in the difficult things. I am excited about our future together.

Never				Sometimes					Always
1	2	3	4	5	6	7	8	9	10

Joyful: We do more together than just the necessities–we create time for each other and we laugh together.

Never				Sometimes					Always
1	2	3	4	5	6	7	8	9	10

Covenantal: I am confident that, through God's grace, we will uphold our marriage covenant.

Never				Sometimes					Always
1	2	3	4	5	6	7	8	9	10

Session Two

Love Protects

Adventure, Laughter, Celebration, Attraction, Connection

Chapters 6 – 10

So far, your experiments have ushered in joy and creativity and brought some surprises into your marriage. But how do you preserve the spark you've worked to create?

You *protect* that spark! You've had some practice being the initiator of romance in your relationship. How do you feel about being a "protector," too? Maybe you've been told that the husband is supposed to be your protector, so it feels strange to assign yourself that kind of responsibility. Maybe you can't envision yourself as the protector of your marriage or, even weirder, as *his* protector. Well, the truth is that you, his wife, are in a better position than any other human to offer him protection. Also, "protecting" might look different than the associations that spring immediately into your mind. Check out the experiments in this section, and you'll see what we mean. With God's help, you can give your husband the protection that he needs.

Let's take the spirit of the experiment even further—with experiments of adventure, laughter, celebration, attraction, and connection.

Chapter 6

RECAP: ADVENTURE

Lisa and Matt—who've been married for decades—left some of the opportunity for adventure behind when they started raising their family and then caregiving for Matt's parents. Lisa knew that even though he hadn't been on an adventure in a while, Matt was certainly an adventurer at heart. Inspired by a joyful older couple who were willing to try new things into their seventies, Lisa experimented with a spontaneous (and reasonable) adventure that she could share with Matt.

"Except once we started raising our children . . . and then caregiving for both of his parents, those things put a bit of a damper on the adventurous life. Sure, Matt still enjoyed dreaming, studying, and watching documentaries of fascinating places and ancient architecture, but that was hardly the same thrill as going there." (From *The Flirtation Experiment*, pages 31 - 32)

How would you gauge the spirit of adventure in your marriage? What do you see as your obstacles to adventure? Have you replaced "real adventures" with something else—like dreaming, studying, and watching? Have you found yourself in a season of "waiting until it gets easier"?

The steadfast love of the Lord never ceases;
his mercies never come to an end;

they are new every morning;
great is your faithfulness. (Lamentations 3:22–23 ESV)

Father God, Your mercies are new every morning—You are always doing something new in my heart, always taking risks to love me. I want to bring that spirit of renewal into my marriage.

MY {ADVENTURE} EXPERIMENT

Brainstorming: What scale of adventure matches your season? If you are spending time and energy parenting and caregiving, or if money feels tight, keep the scale small. Adventure is all in the spirit of the activity. Borrow bikes and take an afternoon ride—even through your own neighborhood! Or, go big! What have you always wanted to try?

My Plan: Pick ONE specific action for your {Adventure} experiment.

WHAT I'm going to do:

WHEN I'm going to do it:

Anything I need to prepare in advance:

My {Adventure} Experiment Reflection:

What Happened:

List a few things about your {Adventure} Experiment that . . .

Encouraged You:	*Disappointed you:*	*Surprised you:*

Our Obstacles:

His Response:

MY {ADVENTURE} EXPERIMENT WRAP-UP

To Ponder: Have you ever met a couple like John and Susan, the couple that Lisa describes in the chapter? They challenged Lisa's expectations about the type of people who can enjoy new adventures–after all, they were in their seventies! What kinds of expectations do you place on adventure–what kind of attributes would a truly "adventurous" person have? Do you–or your husband–have those attributes?

More {Adventure}: Experimenting often requires research! Even if your time of life demands smaller scale adventures, start thinking big! What exotic place would you want to visit? What activity have you always wanted to try? Do a little research. Try to think beyond the financial piece–you're planting seeds for a future adventure, *not* booking a trip right now. What skills would you need to learn? What knowledge would be helpful? Is there a step–even a tiny one–that you could take toward that adventure today, even if it's just placing a book on hold at the library?

Preparing For Your Next Experiment: Think about a recent time your husband made you laugh–what was it that he did? Do you think of him as funny, or is he more of a serious type?

Chapter 7

RECAP: LAUGHTER

Phylicia discovered early on in her relationship with Josh that she didn't laugh only when she thought something was truly funny or she felt happy. She used her laughter to make others–and herself–more comfortable in awkward situations. But she held back laughter when it came to Josh and his jokes. Humor was another place in their relationship that Phylicia felt called to push past the awkwardness and try something that felt a little unnatural. Little by little, she started joking more with Josh. Her willingness to experiment with laughter ushered more of God's joy into their marriage.

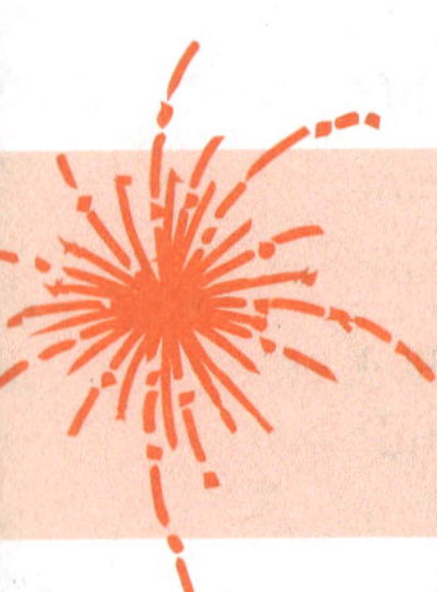

"I was willing to laugh with an acquaintance because he wasn't linked to me, willing to do my social duty of making him feel welcome (bad jokes and all). But when it came to Josh, laughing was off the table." (From *The Flirtation Experiment*, page 38)

Think about it: Why do you laugh? Have you ever experienced what Phylicia writes about, that "social duty" to make other people feel comfortable by laughing? Do you laugh with your husband? Of course, you don't want to laugh at him just because you feel like you have to–but are you willing (at the expense of your pride) to be silly with him?

> You make known to me the path of life;
> in your presence there is fullness of joy;
> at your right hand are pleasures forevermore. (Psalm 16:11 ESV)

God, make known to us the path of life. Your path leads to joy–please help me to foster real laughter in my relationship with my husband. Please take away whatever it is that guards me from truly enjoying him for who he is.

MY {LAUGHTER} EXPERIMENT

Brainstorming: Laughter isn't about being a stand-up comedian–laughter is about invitations and responses. When your husband tells a silly joke (if he does that kind of thing), he's looking for a response from you–and not a response of derision. How could you respond to him in the spirit of the joke?

My Plan: Pick ONE specific action for your {Laughter} experiment.

WHAT I'm going to do:

WHEN I'm going to do it:

Anything I need to prepare in advance:

MY {LAUGHTER} EXPERIMENT REFLECTION:

What Happened:

List a few things about your {Laughter} Experiment that . . .

Encouraged You:	*Disappointed you:*	*Surprised you:*

Our Obstacles:

His Response:

MY {LAUGHTER} EXPERIMENT WRAP-UP

To Ponder: Phylicia cut straight to the heart of the laughter issue when she wrote, "The longer I thought about it, the truth became clear: I was afraid of making other people feel bad. But I also didn't want my own fiancé's puns to reflect on me." Laughing at Josh's jokes required her to risk her own pride. What does laughter put at stake for you–your pride? Your poise or position? Are you willing to risk those things to allow more laughter to enter your marriage?

More {Laughter}: In every marriage, laughter has the potential to bring spouses closer together and draw them deeper into the joy that God longs for us to have in his presence. But every marriage is different–do you have similar senses of humor or different ones? Do you find the same kinds of things funny? Even if you don't, don't worry! You can still laugh together–maybe your senses of humor will even change over time in response to each other! But it's good to have a knowledge baseline.

Preparing For Your Next Experiment: When your husband tells you about a recent success–in any arena of his life–what's your natural response? Are you the type to praise quickly or to wait until you have more information?

Celebration

Chapter 8

RECAP: CELEBRATION

Lisa was devasted when Matt didn't respond joyfully to her great news–she had just made a huge step in her book publishing journey. It looked like she had landed a deal with the perfect company. Her friends were over the moon with her, but Matt didn't say anything at all! She was very hurt.

> "And so I went from a thankful 'Praise the Lord!' that morning to a raging 'What is wrong with that man?' by afternoon. Have you ever taken that journey? Doesn't take much time, does it? I was no longer focused on this marvelous answer to prayer; all I could think about was how much my husband's (lack of) response stole my joy." (From *The Flirtation Experiment*, page 44)

Have you ever raced from "Praise the Lord" to "What is wrong with that man?" in the space of a single day? Describe the situation. What great thing happened to you? How were you expecting your husband to respond, and what did he actually do? How did you feel after his response–both towards him, and about the great thing that had happened?

> "'It was right that we should make merry and be glad, for your brother was dead and is alive again, and was lost and is found.'" (Luke 15:32, NKJV)

God, you celebrate us. You rejoice over us. It is right that we should make merry and be glad. Help me to protect my marriage relationship by celebrating all that you would have us celebrate.

MY {CELEBRATION} EXPERIMENT

Brainstorming: What gifts has God given to you? A celebration recognizes something wonderful. Maybe you made it through another round of potty training–celebrate! Maybe one of you received a promotion–celebrate that! Like adventure, celebration is about spirit, *not* scale.

My Plan: Pick ONE specific action for your {Celebration} experiment.

WHAT I'm going to do:

WHEN I'm going to do it:

Anything I need to prepare in advance:

MY {CELEBRATION} EXPERIMENT REFLECTION:

What Happened:

List a few things about your {Celebration} Experiment that . . .

Encouraged You:	*Disappointed you:*	*Surprised you:*

Our Obstacles:

His Response:

MY {CELEBRATION} EXPERIMENT WRAP-UP

To Ponder: At least in Lisa and Matt's case, Matt had a pretty good reason for not popping open a champagne bottle right away to celebrate Lisa's news. Have you ever found yourself disappointed in your husband's reaction, only to realize later that there was a reason behind his reaction, or lack thereof? Have you ever been the one with what he interpreted as a disappointing reaction?

More {Celebration}: Gratitude is the precursor of any celebration. Especially if you're having a hard time with this experiment, try to think of ten (or even twenty!) reasons to celebrate, preferably events or answered prayers that happened within the last six months. Even if you don't celebrate each of these individually, thank God for each one of these.

This exercise–although I'm sure you've done it before!–will get your mind and heart in celebration mode. Take an honest inventory of all of the good things–of the abundance God has given you.

____

____

____

____

Preparing For Your Next Experiment: Do you remember the first time you saw your husband? What–if anything–stood out to you about him?

____

____

____

Chapter 9

RECAP: ATTRACTION

Phylicia and Josh's first meeting would not have inspired any rom-com screenplays–neither of them left the parking lot where they met with stars in their eyes. Their attraction to each other was built slowly over time. Their relationship was the result of their choice, not an irresistible pull of chemistry. Phylicia discovered that the link between choice and attraction held true for marriage, too. She could choose to find aspects and attributes of Josh's character and behavior that were attractive to her. The attraction experiment was about taking the time to notice those attractive things.

> "And we were right: the better we knew each other, the more we found to admire. And the more we admired each other's character, the more attracted we became." (From *The Flirtation Experiment*, page 50)

What elements of attraction were there when you first met your husband, or when you first got married? What natural elements of attraction were there from the beginning? What have you learned to admire over time?

His head is the finest gold;
his locks are wavy,
black as a raven.
His eyes are like doves
beside streams of water,
bathed in milk,
sitting beside a full pool. (Song of Solomon 5:11–12 ESV)

Lord God, my willingness to be attracted to my husband protects our marriage covenant. Please help me find specific things to admire. Open my eyes, help me to see how You are working in his life.

MY {ATTRACTION} EXPERIMENT

Brainstorming: The lover and the beloved in the Song of Solomon speak intimately about very specific things they admire about one another. Find things to admire about him–keep a list if it helps, maybe just for one day. Be as specific as you can. What actions, words, and appearances attract you to him?

My Plan: Pick ONE specific action for your {Attraction} experiment.

WHAT I'm going to do:

WHEN I'm going to do it:

Anything I need to prepare in advance:

MY {ATTRACTION} EXPERIMENT REFLECTION:

What Happened:

List a few things about your {Attraction} Experiment that . . .

Encouraged You:	*Disappointed you:*	*Surprised you:*

Our Obstacles:

His Response:

MY {ATTRACTION} EXPERIMENT WRAP-UP

To Ponder: Unrealistic expectations about chemistry in marriage come from all directions–from bad teaching, from Hollywood, from other people, and even from ourselves! Phylicia talks about chemistry in marriage as something that needs to be cultivated. Have you ever thought that your own marriage lacked chemistry, either compared to what it used to be or compared to what you thought other people experienced in marriage?

More {Attraction}: The experiment focused on finding things about him to be attracted to–but attraction goes two ways! You are more likely to feel attracted to him if you are feeling attractive yourself. In the chapter, Phylicia mentions putting on make-up and finding beautiful clothing that was comfortable enough for her to wear postpartum. We're all different, though–think about different practices (they can be pretty simple ones!) that make you feel attractive.

Preparing For Your Next Experiment: Think about the time that you and your husband spend together–with just the two of you, not with anyone else! What do you spend the bulk of that time together doing? (This question is not about putting down the "right" answer–just the real one!)

Chapter 10

RECAP: CONNECTION

Lisa and Matt had plenty of reasons to feel burned out, and they found some solace in watching a few shows together before they went to bed. This habit replaced other evening activities–reading, playing games, having conversations. Even though they were in the same room, Lisa found herself missing time with Matt–time that had been replaced with screen time because both of them were stretched so thin. She found a way to connect again in a meaningful way that didn't cost as much energy as reading out loud or having a deep conversation–a board game both of them knew and liked.

"A while back, I heard an online writer friend talk about how she and her husband, while navigating rough waters in their community, had taken to show-binging in bed until they fell asleep. I didn't say anything to her back then, but I now confess that I silently disapproved of such a seeming waste of time." (From *The Flirtation Experiment*, page 60)

Have you ever found yourself in a less-than-ideal habit pattern, or found yourself spending a lot of time as a couple doing an activity that you don't really value? Was there something that preceded settling into that pattern, habit, or activity–like burnout from caregiving, unrest in your community, or stress in your marriage?

____

____

____

And Adam said:

"This *is* now bone of my bones
And flesh of my flesh;
She shall be called Woman,
Because she was taken out of Man." (Genesis 2:23 NKJV)

Father God, Your design for us is for each other, for deep, true, and meaningful connection. What can I do to live into my identity as the "bone of his bones" and "flesh of his flesh"?

MY {CONNECTION} EXPERIMENT

Brainstorming: Meaningful connection doesn't have to mean extensive amounts of time and energy. Go for a twenty-minute walk. Or create playlists and choose songs to play for each other. Maybe you could come up with a fun dessert idea to share–even if it's just something you buy from the store!

My Plan: Pick ONE specific action for your {Connection} experiment.

WHAT I'm going to do:

WHEN I'm going to do it:

Anything I need to prepare in advance:

MY {CONNECTION} EXPERIMENT REFLECTION:

What Happened:

List a few things about your {Connection} Experiment that . . .

Encouraged You:	*Disappointed you:*	*Surprised you:*

Our Obstacles:

His Response:

MY {CONNECTION} EXPERIMENT WRAP-UP

To Ponder: Lisa writes, "I've discovered that it's often the woman who strongly pursues that 'drawing near,' proactively suggesting positive ways to connect." Do you wait for him to initiate moments of connection? Do you ever find yourself disappointed when he doesn't seem interested in initiating during what you would call a "good moment"? Think about the possibility that taking the initiative on connection is a way for you to protect your marriage. Is there any reason you can't reach out to him in the ways that you long for him to reach out to you?

More {Connection}: Near the end of the chapter, Lisa says that, at least in her marriage, it's much better to suggest a change that's already prepped (like the Scrabble game on the table) rather than give her husband a rationale behind why things have to change. Have you ever given your husband "an hour of tearful thoughts" and been underwhelmed by the results? Or is he the kind that needs to talk through changes before they start to happen?

Preparing For Your Next Experiment: Think–briefly–about any weaknesses or struggles you are dealing with now. Which ones does your husband know about? Are there any that you think he wouldn't be able to understand?

Love Protects

ADVENTURE, LAUGHTER, CELEBRATION, ATTRACTION, CONNECTION

Did those experiments match up with your previous concept of "protection"? Did you realize that protecting your husband and your marriage covenant could be as simple as being willing to try something new (we said simple, not easy!)? As being unafraid of looking silly? As combing through the calendar through the "daily stuff" and finding good things to celebrate with him? Finding him attractive and initiating moments of connection are great places to start in your role as his protector.

Rate yourself on these scales of one to ten, one being "Never," five being "Sometimes" and ten being "Always." Go with your first instinct, not with what you think you are supposed to say.

NOTE: if this tracker isn't helpful, DON'T USE IT. This is an opportunity to take an honest look at yourself–not to judge or condemn yourself.

Intentional: I take specific actions to strengthen our marriage and show him that I love him.

Never				Sometimes					Always
1	2	3	4	5	6	7	8	9	10

Faithful: I am a safe place for him. I do not mock him or call him names. He can tell me things and be confident that I won't tell everyone else.

Never				Sometimes					Always
1	2	3	4	5	6	7	8	9	10

Hopeful: I am grateful for our past and I see redemption in it, even in the difficult things. I am excited about our future together.

Never				Sometimes					Always
1	2	3	4	5	6	7	8	9	10

Joyful: We do more together than just the necessities–we create time for each other and we laugh together.

Never				Sometimes					Always
1	2	3	4	5	6	7	8	9	10

Covenantal: I am confident that, through God's grace, we will uphold our marriage covenant.

Never				Sometimes					Always
1	2	3	4	5	6	7	8	9	10

Session Three

Love Trusts

Vulnerability, Mystery, Affirmation, Refuge, Friendship

Chapters 11 – 15

We have covered so much ground together through these experiments. We've definitely hit "awkward" and "uncomfortable" at least a few times by now. Those feelings are part and parcel of the Flirtation Experiment! Like Phylicia said, "I had to recognize that feeling awkward isn't the end of the world; it's the beginning of growth." You've probably had to make peace with that awkward feeling too!

We've asked you to cast yourself in the roles of the initiator, the protector, even the *pursuer* in your marriage. You've fostered joy in your marriage and protected that joy. We're going to keep building on the growth that has begun as we look at the next five experiments: vulnerability, mystery, affirmation, refuge, and friendship. These experiments are all opportunities to trust your husband more deeply and to allow him to entrust himself to you.

Do you trust him?

For that matter, do you trust Him?

No matter what your answers to those questions might be, ask God to help you grow in trust as you carry out these next five experiments.

Chapter 11

RECAP: VULNERABILITY

Phylicia suffered through nightmares each postpartum, but the third time around was especially intense. She had never shared her struggle with Josh, but she didn't really have a choice this time. He kept noticing when she woke up, and, finally, she let him know what was really happening. After she confessed what she had classified as a weakness, Josh comforted her and prayed over her. She took the risk of being vulnerable, and he helped relieve the weight of the burden.

"But I've discovered in the few years that I've been married that Josh wants to be invited into my vulnerable places. Seeing my weakness doesn't push him away; it actually invites him to be strong." (From *The Flirtation Experiment*, page 65)

Is your husband invited into your vulnerable places? Or are you afraid that your weakness will push him away? Are you afraid that he won't respect you or hear you out? How do you feel about the idea that your vulnerability is an invitation for him to be strong?

"Husbands, love your wives, just as Christ also loved the church and gave Himself for her, that He might sanctify and cleanse her with the washing of water by the word, that He might present her to Himself a glorious church, not having spot or wrinkle or any such thing, but that she should be holy and without blemish." (Ephesians 5:25–27 NKJV)

Lord God, when I am vulnerable with my husband, I allow him the opportunity to love me as Christ loved the church. Sometimes I'm afraid to give so much to him–help me to entrust myself to him.

MY {VULNERABILITY} EXPERIMENT

Brainstorming: If being vulnerable with your husband is an unfamiliar exercise, make a specific plan for this experiment. Find a time when you'd have his full attention, then share something with him that he hasn't heard you say before. Plan ahead about what dream, fear, or burden you'll share with him.

My Plan: Pick ONE specific action for your {Vulnerability} experiment.

WHAT I'm going to do:

WHEN I'm going to do it:

Anything I need to prepare in advance:

MY {VULNERABILITY} EXPERIMENT REFLECTION:

What Happened:

List a few things about your {Vulnerability} Experiment that . . .

Encouraged You:	*Disappointed you:*	*Surprised you:*

Our Obstacles:

His Response:

MY {VULNERABILITY} EXPERIMENT WRAP-UP

To Ponder: When it comes to sharing your hopes and fears, who is your "go-to" person? For many of us, the people we trust with our deepest feelings and thoughts are not our husbands. It's great to surround our marriages with supportive people, like friends and family, but it's important to give husbands some priority. Can you think of anything specific that holds you back from trusting him with vulnerable dreams and fears? Or, if you are in the practice of sharing deeply with him, how did you form that practice?

More {Vulnerability}: Phylicia closes out this chapter with this call to action: "Your husband's prayers have great power in your life. Prayer is a vulnerable practice, but when we open the door to vulnerability in marriage, it is often reciprocated." Do you and your husband pray for each other regularly? Have you asked him to pray over you before? What is that experience like for you?

Preparing For Your Next Experiment: Think about an event that you had to plan ahead for, one that you had some responsibility for enacting–it doesn't have to involve your husband. How did you feel about that event in the ten minutes before it was supposed to start?

Chapter 12

RECAP: MYSTERY

For once, Lisa knew that Matt would be surprised. She planned out a mystery date for the two of them, complete with changes of scenery and dinner reservations. Throughout the day, she was going to give him hints on notecards, making the date an all-day affair. But before she handed him the first card, she totally froze. She pushed through the thought, "This is a terrible idea!" She was glad she did, because Matt loved the date–especially the mysterious elements.

"No, I wasn't done berating myself as I sat paralyzed in my chair. The "stupid" list continued like the end of a drum solo that won't stop. I now thought of everything that was so obviously wrong with my plan." (From *The Flirtation Experiment*, page 70)

Have you ever made a great plan, maybe for a trip or a date, and then found yourself totally flustered right before you were supposed to take the first step? Did you manage to talk yourself out of it, or did you go through with it? How did it end up going?

> Three things are too wondrous for me;
> four I can't understand:
> the way of an eagle in the sky,
> the way of a snake on a rock,
> the way of a ship at sea,
> and the way of a man with a young woman. (Proverbs 30:18–19 CSB)

God, marriage is the celebration of a wonderful mystery–the way of a man with a woman. Help me embrace the mystery in my marriage. Help me wonder at how Christ loves Your church.

MY {MYSTERY} EXPERIMENT

Brainstorming: Experiment a little with mystery: plan out an evening with him–make sure he knows that you'll be doing something, but keep all of the details mysterious. If you're up for a real challenge, bring some other couples into the experiment for a murder mystery dinner.

My Plan: Pick ONE specific action for your {Mystery} experiment.

WHAT I'm going to do:

WHEN I'm going to do it:

Anything I need to prepare in advance:

MY {MYSTERY} EXPERIMENT REFLECTION:

What Happened:

List a few things about your {Mystery} Experiment that . . .

Encouraged You:	*Disappointed you:*	*Surprised you:*

Our Obstacles:

His Response:

MY {MYSTERY} EXPERIMENT WRAP-UP

To Ponder: Lisa writes about her mystery date, "The planning really was easy. What I didn't anticipate was that initial morning panic." It's very possible that your mystery plan will be accompanied by some panic, especially right before "go-time." What could you do to push past that feeling that Lisa talks about the "this is so stupid!" feeling? What's really behind that panic–the fear of failure? Difficulty embracing unknowns?

More {Mystery}: Paul writes about marriage in his letter to the Ephesians, "This mystery is profound, and I am saying that it refers to Christ and the church" (5:32 ESV). Spend some time praying with this verse. Maybe read the rest of the chapter for some more context on Paul's thoughts on marriage. Would you describe your own marriage as "mysterious"? Or does it feel strange to assign that word to a relationship that has so many pedestrian elements–like dishes, and bills, and quiet evenings at home?

Preparing For Your Next Experiment: Generally speaking, when you consider a situation, is it easier for you to think through what's going well or what could be improved?

Chapter 13

RECAP: AFFIRMATION

The air was tense between Phylicia and Josh during the weeks after their third baby was born. Amid the diapers and the feeding and the care for the older children, Phylicia realized that criticism was flowing pretty freely, but she wasn't taking the time to affirm Josh. She reoriented her own thoughts, choosing to notice all of the things that Josh was doing right. She ended up sending him a letter of affirmation, but the difference started to take effect when she reigned in her own thoughts.

> **"All I saw was room for improvement. I mulled on his transgressions until they became a veritable stew of offenses in my mind: *he should have; why didn't he? I wish he'd . . ."* (From *The Flirtation Experiment*, page 78)**

When you consider your husband's actions and his character, do you ever find yourself rehashing the things he does wrong? Are there any particular triggers for these kinds of negative thought cycles? Phylicia narrowed in on negative things about Josh during postpartum. Are there seasons or situations that seem to be fertile grounds for negative thoughts about him?

____

____

____

____

____

____

"Finally, brothers, whatever is true, whatever is honorable, whatever is just, whatever is pure, whatever is lovely, whatever is commendable, if there is any excellence, if there is anything worthy of praise, think about these things." (Philippians 4:8 ESV)

Father God, I want to think about my husband in ways that are honoring to You and to our marriage covenant. Help me to focus on things honorable, commendable, and excellent about him.

MY {AFFIRMATION} EXPERIMENT

Brainstorming: This experiment really has two parts: noticing praiseworthy things about your husband, and then actually praising (or affirming) him. Plan out how you're going to affirm him–are you going to write a letter and read it out loud? Or write a note and leave it by his chair? Be creative!

My Plan: Pick ONE specific action for your {Affirmation} experiment.

WHAT I'm going to do:

WHEN I'm going to do it:

Anything I need to prepare in advance:

MY {AFFIRMATION} EXPERIMENT REFLECTION:

What Happened:

List a few things about your {Affirmation} Experiment that . . .

Encouraged You:	*Disappointed you:*	*Surprised you:*

Our Obstacles:

His Response:

MY {AFFIRMATION} EXPERIMENT WRAP-UP

To Ponder: Love trusts, and trust flourishes in an environment of affirmation. Phylicia writes, "What we affirm in our husbands can build trust in our counsel or can make him feel like we don't like him at all." Affirming your husband helps him trust you. Of course, you have to take a step in trust to even give him affirmations. Do you have any fears or worries that he won't receive affirmation from you, either in your experiment or in the future? Is it difficult to trust him with your affirming words?

More {Affirmation}: Phylicia notes that the change in her thought patterns wasn't instantaneous–it took work and observations. She started by acknowledging the negative thoughts about Josh when they came up and then following those thoughts up with positive, affirming thoughts. Do you find that you need to gradually switch into a mode of affirmation, or does noticing the good come easily to you?

Preparing For Your Next Experiment: Describe–just in a few sentences–your husband's childhood. Think of him as a young boy, between eight and twelve. Where did he live? What did he like to do? Who took care of him?

Chapter 14

RECAP: REFUGE

Lisa and her children loved listening to Matt talk about his adventurous childhood in the backcountry of British Colombia. She even felt jealous of all the freedom he grew up with. One day, it hit her–ten-year-old Matt must have felt unsafe and alone in the wilderness. At a good time, she questioned him about it–how did all of that freedom really make him feel? Matt's answer was honest–he felt like a lost boy. Lisa reassured Matt that their marriage was a refuge for him.

"For some years I was puzzled by certain aspects of Matt's way of being. Someone could drive a truck through the living room and he wouldn't flinch but would only be concerned that no one was hurt. Conversely, something that seemed so small to me triggered a visceral response in him." (From *The Flirtation Experiment*, page 84)

Have you ever felt confused by some of your husband's responses to daily happenings? Are there things–like meals, or trips, or celebrations–that seem to cause him difficulties that you don't resonate with or understand? Have you considered the possibility that some of his childhood experiences could be influencing his reactions and mannerisms?

"Trust in Him at all times, you people;
Pour out your heart before Him;
God is a refuge for us." (Psalm 62:8, NKJV)

Heavenly Father, You are the refuge for both of us and for our marriage. Within that strength of Your refuge, help us to be a refuge for each other. We want to trust in You at all times.

MY {REFUGE} EXPERIMENT

Brainstorming: Come up with a way to tell your husband that you are a refuge for him. This doesn't have to be a long conversation–but you could make the environment memorable, creating a spot where the two of you can sit close together. What could you do that reinforces the idea of "sanctuary"?

My Plan: Pick ONE specific action for your {Refuge} experiment.

WHAT I'm going to do:

WHEN I'm going to do it:

Anything I need to prepare in advance:

MY {REFUGE} EXPERIMENT REFLECTION:

What Happened:

List a few things about your {Refuge} Experiment that . . .

Encouraged You:	*Disappointed you:*	*Surprised you:*

Our Obstacles:

His Response:

MY {REFUGE} EXPERIMENT WRAP-UP

To Ponder: Not everyone's childhood was like Matt's, of course–in the good ways or the bad ones! But your husband certainly had experiences that made him feel unsafe, unloved, and unprotected. Can you think of ways that he, as a child or a young adult, was left lonely or under protected? Were there times or situations that called for an older person to take responsibility for him? Whether that person was unable to step up or chose not to take responsibility, how was your husband affected?

More {Refuge}: Lisa writes, "A refuge is a sanctuary—a place where mercy is extended and grace is offered." Are there any aspects of your husband's character or pieces of his past toward which you don't want to extend mercy or offer grace? Pray over these difficult and tender places, keeping in mind that image of your husband as a little boy, a boy who sometimes felt lost and unprotected. Ask God to give you His compassion and to grow in you the desire to be your husband's refuge.

Preparing For Your Next Experiment: Would you call your husband your best friend?

Chapter 15

RECAP: FRIENDSHIP

Phylicia and Josh associated "friendship" and "marriage" in completely different ways, a clash of expectations which resulted in hurt feelings from all directions after they got married. Phylicia had no desire to be married to her best friend–she zealously guarded her independence. And Josh? He wanted to be wanted and to feel like Phylicia depended on him. Slowly, Phylicia came around to the idea that friendship in marriage didn't have to mean codependency. Through making time for togetherness, Phylicia and Josh made room for friendship in their marriage and made a pathway toward forgiveness for each other for those first difficult years.

"To marry your best friend meant losing all other ones, and I wanted none of that. I wanted marriage, but I also wanted to preserve my independence—at all costs." (From *The Flirtation Experiment*, page 90)

Are you like Phylicia–do you find the idea of "marrying your best friend" totally suffocating and bent toward codependency? Or do you long for friendship with your husband? Maybe you are already enjoying a friendship with your husband–how are the elements of that friendship different than your other friendships?

"Greater love has no one than this, that someone lay down his life for his friends." (John 15:13 ESV)

Lord God, You laid down your life for me. You risked everything for friendship with me. Help me to keep building friendship with my husband, a friendship that finds its foundation in Your willingness to call me "friend."

MY {FRIENDSHIP} EXPERIMENT

Brainstorming: Friendship can be described as that "me too!" feeling–what creates that feeling in your marriage? For Phylicia and Josh, it's skiing. For you and your husband, it might be music, or a sports team, or a favorite place. How could you invest some time and resources into that shared interest?

My Plan: Pick ONE specific action for your {Friendship} experiment.

WHAT I'm going to do:

WHEN I'm going to do it:

Anything I need to prepare in advance:

MY {FRIENDSHIP} EXPERIMENT REFLECTION:

What Happened:

List a few things about your {Friendship} Experiment that . . .

Encouraged You:	*Disappointed you:*	*Surprised you:*

Our Obstacles:

His Response:

MY {FRIENDSHIP} EXPERIMENT WRAP-UP

To Ponder: As Phylicia found out, "laying down your life" can also mean "surrendering your independence." This doesn't mean depending on each other in unhealthy ways–it means being willing to need each other. Think of it as interdependent rather than codependent. Are there certain areas of your life in which you are still adamant about your independence–maybe the finances, or maybe a hobby, even a certain household chore? As weird as it sounds, pray about what "laying down your life" would look like in that area where you demand independence–whatever it might be.

More {Friendship}: Phylicia writes, "This kind of friendship can happen even without those peripheral interests. It's a friendship based on love for *the person himself.* It's a reminder of who he is as an image bearer of God." To present yourself to your husband you are–just as yourself–is an extreme exercise in trust. Especially if you feel like there's not much going on in your marriage in the way of shared interests, take some time to acknowledge that what you have in common is each other–your one-ness as a couple, and the image of God that each of you bears to the other.

Preparing For Your Next Experiment: How do you react when your husband walks into a room? Could someone else who didn't know you tell that you were married?

Session Three Conclusion:

Love Trusts

VULNERABILITY, MYSTERY, AFFIRMATION, REFUGE, FRIENDSHIP

Hopefully, you took advantage of the many chances that those experiments offered you to grow in trust in your marriage. You were challenged to be vulnerable with your husband, sharing with him something you'd never shared before. You were asked to play around with the idea of mystery, and to offer him affirmations without knowing how he would respond. You told him that you were both his refuge and his friend, offering him both deep trust and entrustment of your person. Can you feel any shifts or changes in your marriage at this point?

Rate yourself on these scales of one to ten, one being "Never," five being "Sometimes" and ten being "Always.

Go with your first instinct, not with what you think you are supposed to say.

NOTE: If this tracker isn't helpful, DON'T USE IT. This is about honest time for reflection–not condemnation or judgment of yourself.

Intentional: I take specific actions to strengthen our marriage and show him that I love him.

Never Sometimes Always

1	2	3	4	5	6	7	8	9	10

Faithful: I am a safe place for him. I do not mock him or call him names. He can tell me things and be confident that I won't tell everyone else.

Never Sometimes Always

1	2	3	4	5	6	7	8	9	10

Hopeful: I am grateful for our past and I see redemption in it, even in the difficult things. I am excited about our future together.

Never				Sometimes					Always
1	2	3	4	5	6	7	8	9	10

Joyful: We do more together than just the necessities–we create time for each other and we laugh together.

Never				Sometimes					Always
1	2	3	4	5	6	7	8	9	10

Covenantal: I am confident that, through God's grace, we will uphold our marriage covenant.

Never				Sometimes					Always
1	2	3	4	5	6	7	8	9	10

Session Four

Love Hopes

Delight, Respect, Romance, Intimacy, Blessing

Chapters 16 – 20

Love always hopes. Love is able to find what is good in the present and look forward with anticipation into the future. Love is able to part peacefully with the past, all the while asserting that the best is yet to come. Love is not overcome by anxiety or by the complexity of everyday details.

These next experiments give you the opportunity to bring hope into your marriage in the places that it needs it the most. The strongest hopes turn up in very unexpected places–in that conversation that you've been circling around for years, in that problem that never seems to be solved, in that trial that turned your future in a direction you never expected it to go. Ask God to help you hope again, particularly in that arena of life or place in marriage that you've just stopped hoping will improve. Then, get ready to grow through the next experiments–experiments of delight, respect, romance, intimacy, and blessing.

Chapter 16

RECAP: DELIGHT

When they first met, Matt and Lisa fell head over heels for each other–Lisa couldn't help but smile when she remembered how she used to react when he walked into the room. After watching a new wife beam at her husband when he came into church, Lisa realized that she didn't "light up" for Matt on purpose anymore. They both knew it–the way that she reacted to his presence had changed over time. So Lisa decided to experiment with her delight in Matt, with her immediate reaction toward him, to see if the conscious choice to delight in him made any difference.

"So what happened to that young woman who was me? Nothing—and *everything*. Daily life, babies and homeschooling, music lessons and ministry meetings, breakfast, lunch, and dinner. Somehow it had all stacked up, and without my even realizing it, I'd stopped smiling *like that*". (From *The Flirtation Experiment*, page 97)

Chances are, when you first met your husband, your list of responsibilities looked different. Even if you've only been married a short time, your schedule has probably changed from when you were dating him. What's your answer to Lisa's question: What happened to that young woman who was you?

____

____

____

____

Scarcely had I passed them
when I found him whom my soul loves.
I held him, and would not let him go. (Song of Solomon 3:4 ESV)

Heavenly Father, I want to ask you for the gift of delight in my husband. Help me to make the choices that say that he is the one whom my soul loves–the one whom I want to hold and not let go.

MY {DELIGHT} EXPERIMENT

Brainstorming: Delight in your husband isn't about "faking it til you make it"–choosing to show delight isn't fake, even if your feelings need some time to get in gear. Decide what you'll do to communicate "delight" the next time you see him–whether it's a smile, a word of welcome, or an affectionate touch.

My Plan: Pick ONE specific action for your {Delight} experiment.

WHAT I'm going to do:

WHEN I'm going to do it:

Anything I need to prepare in advance:

MY {DELIGHT} EXPERIMENT REFLECTION:

What Happened:

List a few things about your {Delight} Experiment that . . .

Encouraged You:	*Disappointed you:*	*Surprised you:*

Our Obstacles:

His Response:

MY {DELIGHT} EXPERIMENT WRAP-UP

To Ponder: What makes you "light up"? How do you usually communicate your pleasure or approval? When you see something–like a beautiful sunset–or someone–like one of your children and feel delighted, what do you naturally do to show it?

More {Delight}: Maybe you're still concerned about what feels like "faking" delight. You have options there, too! Lisa writes, "Obviously the goal wasn't merely to plaster on a fake smile, but to communicate my true pleasure in him, so this sometimes meant I would spend several minutes reflecting on those things about him that genuinely delighted me." The feeling of "delight" was more easily accessible in the early days. But the passage of time has given you deeper reasons to delight in him. Spend a few minutes thinking about what about your husband truly delights you.

Preparing For Your Next Experiment: Have you ever known anyone that really wanted your respect? You can list your husband here, but think about other relationships, too. What about those people made you want to give them respect (or withhold it from them)?

Chapter 17

RECAP: RESPECT

Phylicia and Josh didn't fit into the typical categories when it came to love and respect. Both of them wanted to be respected *and* loved. Over the course of their marriage, Phylicia discovered that Josh's "respect language" had a lot more to do with attention than accolades. And even though it was not the way that she was used to thinking of respect, Phylicia decided to learn the language. She experimented with a simple but powerful way to let Josh know that she respected him.

> "During our engagement, we had learned that views about men desiring respect and women desiring love were not a full representation of our own relationship. I wanted to be respected, and he wanted affection and attentiveness." (From *The Flirtation Experiment*, page 101)

Can you relate? Look at your own marriage. Do you and your husband fit the "respect and love" paradigm so often circulated in Christian circles–that men want respect and women want love? Paul writes about this in Ephesians (see Ephesians 5:33), but is it possible that those terms are broader than the discussion you've heard about them?

"Let love be without hypocrisy. Detest evil; cling to what is good. Love one another deeply as brothers and sisters. Take the lead in honoring one another." (Romans 12:9–10 CSB)

Lord God, help us to love each other without hypocrisy. Help both of us take the lead in honoring one another, being attentive to the way that each of us receives love and respect.

MY {RESPECT} EXPERIMENT

Brainstorming: You could ask your husband how he receives respect and make an effort to respond to his thoughts, like Phylicia did. Or, if you want this to be more of a surprise, make a list of reasons why you respect him, keeping it simple and to the point. Give it to him and see how he responds.

My Plan: Pick ONE specific action for your {Respect} experiment.

WHAT I'm going to do:

WHEN I'm going to do it:

Anything I need to prepare in advance:

MY {RESPECT} EXPERIMENT REFLECTION:

What Happened:

List a few things about your {Respect} Experiment that . . .

Encouraged You:	*Disappointed you:*	*Surprised you:*

Our Obstacles:

His Response:

MY {RESPECT} EXPERIMENT WRAP-UP

To Ponder: Near the end of the chapter, Phylicia uses the term "loving respect". Treating another person with loving respect first requires having a hopeful attitude about the relationship. Not a "plaster a smile on it" attitude, but a truly hopeful one–an attitude that is built on the belief that your marriage can be a flourishing ground for loving respect that goes both ways. Do you have hope that you and your husband can build on the respect and love for each other that is already there?

More {Respect}: Phylicia writes, "Respect is a lifestyle of honor toward another human being." How does your lifestyle honor your husband? Your parents? Your children, if you have any? What kinds of actions and attitudes contribute to living a "lifestyle of honor"? What kinds of actions and attitudes detract from that lifestyle?

Preparing For Your Next Experiment: Draw a timeline of your marriage–circle the times that were the most romantic.

Chapter 18

RECAP: ROMANCE

Lisa and Matt don't fit the bill of "honeymooners," but Lisa booked a couple nights in a honeymoon cabin, anyway. Lisa's romance experiment meant convincing Matt to steal away for some time together, even though, truth be told, they didn't have "time" for it, and they'd already been together for decades. Having reconciled the idea that a Christian woman can desire romance with her husband and truly live out her role as a wife and mother, Lisa called her beloved out of their daily grind for some time with just each other.

"Time-wise we couldn't afford this mini-honeymoon adventure; it was an exceptionally inconvenient month to schedule a romantic getaway. (Is there ever a convenient time in our fast-paced twenty-first-century world?) Yet I managed to persuade Matt that this was precisely why we should do it." (From *The Flirtation Experiment*, page 108)

Time is a big part of perception of romance–two lovers, totally caught up in each other, are somehow outside the bounds of time. They can spend hours together and not notice that any time has gone by at all. You probably also wonder where the time goes, but not in the same way! Is there time for romance in your marriage–for the two of you to give your undivided attention to each other? What obligations seem to stand in the way of that use of time?

"Therefore a man shall leave his father and mother and be joined to his wife, and they shall become one flesh. And they were both naked, the man and his wife, and were not ashamed." (Genesis 2:24–25 NKJV)

Father God, Adam and Eve were one flesh–naked and unashamed. You gave them each other, and You gave them time for each other. Help us find the time to be with one another, and with you - completely unashamed.

MY {ROMANCE} EXPERIMENT

Brainstorming: Set aside time for your beloved. You could take to the internet and book that trip! If that kind of time and money is totally out of the question, dedicate some hours at home to romance. Have a living room picnic, stargaze from the porch, or bring some coconut oil and candles into the bedroom.

My Plan: Pick ONE specific action for your {Romance} experiment.

WHAT I'm going to do:

WHEN I'm going to do it:

Anything I need to prepare in advance:

MY {ROMANCE} EXPERIMENT REFLECTION:

What Happened:

List a few things about your {Romance} Experiment that . . .

Encouraged You:	*Disappointed you:*	*Surprised you:*

Our Obstacles:

His Response:

MY {ROMANCE} EXPERIMENT WRAP-UP

To Ponder: In respect to "romance," Lisa used to ask herself, "Why would a fairly practical, down-to-earth Christian woman like me long for such impractical, intangible things?" She never put the words "God" and "romance" together. But, like Matt pointed out, the Garden of Eden must have been a haven of romance–nothing held Adam and Eve back from each other. Do you resist the idea of romance? Or do you long for romance but are unsure how it is supposed to fit in to your marriage?

More {Romance}: Near the end of the chapter, Lisa encourages any woman who wants more romance in her marriage to go ahead and make it happen! One of the primary ways that a wife can romance her husband is by carving out enough time for togetherness as a couple. Even though romance doesn't require large amounts of money, it does require some dedicated time. Are there any demands on your time that feel unmovable and draining? Do you trust God with your time–or do you find yourself trying to do everything on your own terms?

Preparing For Your Next Experiment: How does anger manifest in your marriage? How do you express your anger? How does he? Would you say that one of you is more "comfortable" with anger than the other?

____

____

Chapter 19

RECAP: INTIMACY

For years, Phylicia held back her deepest, most intimate longings from Josh. She could be physically intimate with him, but she was terrified of emotional intimacy. When he got too close, she pushed him away with her anger. Her fears were all founded on the belief that, just as she was, she wasn't "enough"–not for Josh, and certainly not for God. This cycle of anger and fear continued until Phylicia was willing to accept that, just as she was, God loved her. She was enough for Him. When she believed this, Phylicia found the strength to hope for and create real intimacy with Josh–an intimacy both of them had been longing for.

"Among other things, anger can be a gut-level response to fear of loss, fear of intimacy, or fear of failure. In my case, I lashed out at Josh whenever I felt like I was failing. Anger is not a welcoming emotion, and my husband naturally pulled away from me." (From *The Flirtation Experiment*, page 114)

What happens when you get angry? Do you withdraw? Or do you lash out? Think about a time that you expressed anger at your husband–what did that look like? Think about a time that he was angry with you–how does he show his anger?

____

____

> "There is no fear in love, but perfect love casts out fear. For fear has to do with punishment, and whoever fears has not been perfected in love." (1 John 4:18 ESV)

Heavenly Father, Your love for us is perfect. Cast the fear out of our hearts with Your great love. Help us to bring all of our fears to You. We want to grow in love, in trust, and in intimacy.

MY {INTIMACY} EXPERIMENT

Brainstorming: Creating intimacy begins with getting inside your own head. Set aside ten minutes (no distractions!) to think about the last time you got angry with your husband–ask God to reveal the underlying reasons for your anger. What was all of that *really* about?

My Plan: Pick ONE specific action for your {Intimacy} experiment.

WHAT I'm going to do:

WHEN I'm going to do it:

Anything I need to prepare in advance:

MY {INTIMACY} EXPERIMENT REFLECTION:

What Happened:

List a few things about your {Intimacy} Experiment that . . .

Encouraged You:	*Disappointed you:*	*Surprised you:*

Our Obstacles:

His Response:

MY {INTIMACY} EXPERIMENT WRAP-UP

To Ponder: For many of us, anger and fear are intricately connected. Maybe anger kicks in because you feel deeply afraid, and you don't want anyone, especially your husband, to know about that fear. Phylicia asks near the end of the chapter, "*What am I afraid of losing when I get angry?*" What's your answer to this question?

More {Intimacy}: True intimacy with your husband is founded on your intimacy with God. Phylicia writes, "Believing that God actually loves you, and that His love changes your life, is the first step to conquering fear. Fear can't be kicked out until Perfect Love walks in." Do you believe that God actually loves you, exactly as you are? What holds you back from this hope?

Preparing For Your Next Experiment: Think about the word "blessing." What actions or mental images come to mind when you think about "blessing" someone or being "blessed"?

Blessing

Chapter 20

RECAP: BLESSING

Lisa wanted to give Matt an excellent gift for his 60th birthday. If she could manage it, the gift wouldn't just surprise him or make him happy, it would truly bless him. Lisa knew Matt loved words, so she gathered notes from family members and friends and compiled them into a beautiful gift. She watched him open and read through all of the notes on his birthday. It was a hundred-fold blessing–an endless list of beautiful words calling out God's favor, grace, and love in Matt's life.

"Uncertain of where to begin, I occasionally placed my hand on my children's heads when I'd walk by them, speaking a short word of blessing—of God's favor on their lives." (From *The Flirtation Experiment*, page 121)

You don't have to be a pastor or an expert to offer a blessing to someone. Lisa started blessing her children by placing her hands on their heads and reminding them of God's love for them. Have you ever done anything like this? Do you have any hesitancy when it comes to offering blessings to your family?

Blessed is the man
Who walks not in the counsel of the ungodly,
Nor stands in the path of sinners,
Nor sits in the seat of the scornful;
But his delight is in the law of the Lord,
And in His law he meditates day and night. (Psalm 1:1–2 NKJV)

Lord God, instead of mocking and scoffing, we can speak words of blessing over each other in Your name. We want to delight in your law and love your law, and meditate on it day and night.

MY {BLESSING} EXPERIMENT

Brainstorming: Plan a blessing for your husband. In some way, speak hopeful words of God's favor into his life. You could offer him a blessing on a date or before he falls asleep. Send it in a text message or write it in a note. If you're nervous about blessing him, write something out! Keep it short and simple.

My Plan: Pick ONE specific action for your {Blessing} experiment.

WHAT I'm going to do:

WHEN I'm going to do it:

Anything I need to prepare in advance:

MY {BLESSING} EXPERIMENT REFLECTION:

What Happened:

List a few things about your {Blessing} Experiment that . . .

Encouraged You:	*Disappointed you:*	*Surprised you:*

Our Obstacles:

His Response:

MY {BLESSING} EXPERIMENT WRAP-UP

To Ponder: Words have tremendous power. Words can build a man up or tear him down. As a wife, you have extraordinary power to bless your husband with hopeful words. What comes to mind when you relate the concept of "words" to your marriage? Does the tone of your general conversation to each other and about each other tilt toward blessing, or do things sometimes go the other direction–towards disparaging, discouraging, or even "cursing"?

More {Blessing}: Lisa writes that saying a blessing can be "something as simple as this: 'I believe God's hand of favor is on you.'" Like any other activity, blessing gets easier with practice. Who else could you bless? Your children? Your mom? Your best friend? Write out a few practice blessings (feel free to keep them short!) in the space below. Speaking words of hope, affirming God's love and favor, can enrich your marriage, but it can enrich your whole community, as well. Ask the Holy Spirit to inspire these words and to give you the courage to speak words of blessings into the lives of the people around you.

Preparing For Your Next Experiment: Write about a memorable "gifting" experience–maybe, one Christmas, you found the perfect gift for someone on your list. What was the best–or worst–gift moment you can remember?

Session Four Conclusion:

Love Hopes

DELIGHT, RESPECT, ROMANCE, INTIMACY, BLESSING

These experiments gave you opportunities to act out of hope–hope in God and in your husband. They also offered invitations to your husband to grow in his hope in God and in you. Delighting in him, respecting him, and romancing him all require you to hope that your husband will respond to you. He might not do it perfectly, or in the way that you expect, but you are certainly putting yourself out there! Becoming more intimate with him and speaking blessing over him are radical exercises in hope.

Rate yourself on these scales of one to ten, one being "Never," five being "Sometimes" and ten being "Always." Go with your first instinct, not with what you think you are supposed to say.

NOTE: If this tracker isn't helpful, DON'T USE IT. This is about honest time for reflection–not condemnation or judgment of yourself.

Intentional: I take specific actions to strengthen our marriage and show him that I love him.

Never Sometimes Always

1 2 3 4 5 6 7 8 9 10

Faithful: I am a safe place for him. I do not mock him or call him names. He can tell me things and be confident that I won't tell everyone else.

Never Sometimes Always

1 2 3 4 5 6 7 8 9 10

Hopeful: I am grateful for our past and I see redemption in it, even in the difficult things. I am excited about our future together.

Never | Sometimes | Always

1	2	3	4	5	6	7	8	9	10

Joyful: We do more together than just the necessities–we create time for each other and we laugh together.

Never | Sometimes | Always

1	2	3	4	5	6	7	8	9	10

Covenantal: I am confident that, through God's grace, we will uphold our marriage covenant.

Never | Sometimes | Always

1	2	3	4	5	6	7	8	9	10

Session Five

Love Perseveres

Generosity, Rest,
Thoughtfulness, Comfort, Faith

Chapters 21 – 25

Can the Flirtation Experiment help us make it through the next really hard time?

What has the Flirtation Experiment done for your marriage so far? Maybe you've been able to rekindle some romance, inspire some laughter, or say something that really needed to be said. Maybe you've learned something about your husband (or yourself!) that you'd never realized before. We hope that "fun" has figured into your Flirtation Experiment in a big way.

But what about the next time you hit a rough patch? The next time one of you loses a job? The next time you face a difficult diagnosis–for one of you, for one of your parents, or even for one of your children? The next time you're both silent and furious in the kitchen, thinking, *"Who is this person that I married?"*

Can the Flirtation Experiment help with something like that?

We think so. Love perseveres and endures through trials–people who love each other are willing to suffer with each other and are willing to continue on together, even when things are harder than they ever thought they could be.

These next experiments–of generosity, rest, thoughtfulness, comfort, and faith–can help both of you live in that truth from Scripture–love *perseveres*.

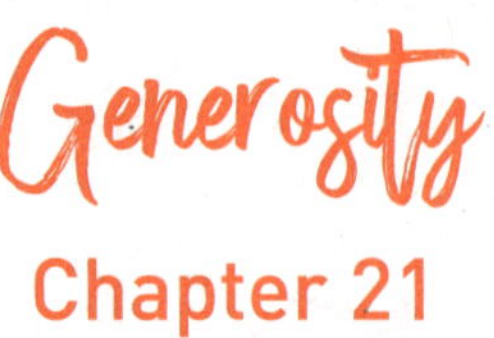

Chapter 21

RECAP: GENEROSITY

Phylicia loved surprising Josh with the perfect gift, but she relegated the idea of "generosity" to objects. It was easy to think of the right gift for him, but she found it incredibly difficult to give Josh an abundance of her time and attention. Eventually, she realized that her lack of generosity was costing both of them in intimacy. She created some firm boundaries–especially with her smartphone–that allowed her to give her time more freely to Josh.

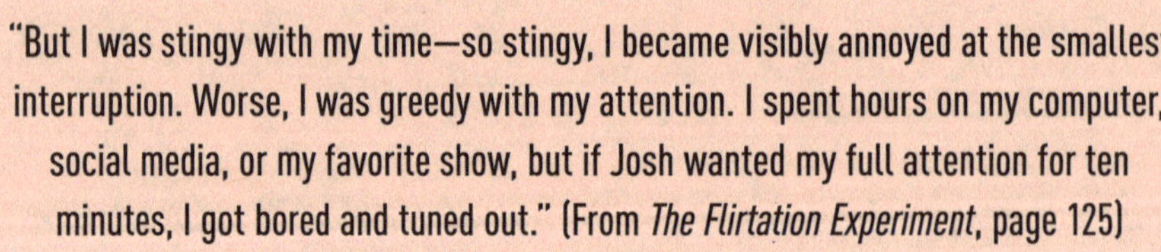

What does the economy of time look like in your marriage? Does one of you desire to have more uninterrupted time together? Does one of you struggle to sacrifice time alone for time together?

____

____

One gives freely, yet grows all the richer;
another withholds what he should give, and only suffers want.

> Whoever brings blessing will be enriched,
> and one who waters will himself be watered. (Proverbs 11:24–25 ESV)

Lord God, when we give to each other freely, we grow rich in Your love. When I withhold time from my husband, or when he withholds it from me, we each suffer in want. Help us give freely.

MY {GENEROSITY} EXPERIMENT

Brainstorming: Consider the role that technology plays in your use of time. What kind of boundaries do you have around your tech–is something always playing in the background? For a day or two, try a different technology routine. Keep it simple. Check back in–were you more free to sacrifice time?

My Plan: Pick ONE specific action for your {Generosity} experiment.

WHAT I'm going to do:

WHEN I'm going to do it:

Anything I need to prepare in advance:

MY {GENEROSITY} EXPERIMENT REFLECTION:

What Happened:

List a few things about your {Generosity} Experiment that . . .

Encouraged You:	*Disappointed you:*	*Surprised you:*

Our Obstacles:

His Response:

MY {GENEROSITY} EXPERIMENT WRAP-UP

To Ponder: About guarding her time, Phylicia wrote, "My stalwart protection of time and attention gave me my space at the cost of our intimacy." Of course, we all need time to ourselves. There is such a thing as a healthy amount of space. But is your "down time" actual rest time? Or does it drain you? Do you find a lot to relate to in that Proverb about withholding what you should give and suffering want? What do you think real rest would look like for you? Do you make time for that real rest?

More {Generosity}: At the end of the chapter, Phylicia writes that she had to change her approach to time first without expecting Josh to change in tandem. It's easy to critique the way that your husband uses his time. But challenge yourself by refusing to look for his faults. This is a great chance for you to take responsibility, to cultivate generosity in your marriage *now*–you never know what trials are on the horizon. Ask God to show you what aspects of your own usage of time honor (or dishonor) Him.

Preparing For Your Next Experiment: When you don't get enough rest, who in your family is the most affected?

Chapter 22

RECAP: REST

Lisa and Matt journeyed together through caregiving for both of his aging parents. Matt's mother died of Alzheimer's, and his father needed hospice care toward the end of his life. After such a long and trying season, the first thing Matt and Lisa needed was rest. It was difficult to say who needed it the most. By prioritizing time for rest, Matt and Lisa protected each other and their marriage.

"When a couple exchanges marriage vows, despite the 'for better, for worse' part, they don't anticipate such an eventuality. We had pictured scenarios of our promises—richer, poorer, sickness, and health—but carrying his lost, naked mother through the fall night back to her own bed was never one of them. Eventually life teaches you that married love doesn't always look like you think it will." (From *The Flirtation Experiment*, page 132)

Even if you haven't been married for very long, you have experienced the dissonance between your expectations for married life and the actuality of married life. This isn't what you thought it would be. Write about an experience in your marriage that challenged you in ways you never thought you'd face.

"Come to me, all who labor and are heavy laden, and I will give you rest. Take my yoke upon you, and learn from me, for I am gentle and lowly in heart, and you will find rest for your souls. For my yoke is easy, and my burden is light." (Matthew 11:28–30 ESV)

Father in Heaven, we need rest for our souls. Your yoke is easy and your burden is light. We cannot rest apart from You. Please help us to take Your yoke upon us and to seek real rest.

MY {REST} EXPERIMENT

Brainstorming: How can you make time for rest? Do you need to commit to an earlier bedtime, even just for a few nights? You could experiment with saying "no" to extra engagements and activities, especially if your default answer is "yes." Maybe both of you need time away–how could you make that happen?

My Plan: Pick ONE specific action for your {Rest} experiment.

WHAT I'm going to do:

WHEN I'm going to do it:

Anything I need to prepare in advance:

MY {REST} EXPERIMENT REFLECTION:

What Happened:

List a few things about your {Rest} Experiment that . . .

Encouraged You:	*Disappointed you:*	*Surprised you:*

Our Obstacles:

His Response:

MY {REST} EXPERIMENT WRAP-UP

To Ponder: Lisa asks, "Who needs rest more: you or your husband?" She followed that up with an unexpected answer: "Likely both." There are a lot of cultural messages out there about husbands being lazy, and about women shouldering the responsibility of "doing it all." As we've seen throughout the Flirtation Experiment, marriage is about both people giving of themselves. Think about the question: "Who needs rest more?" and offer some challenges to the first answer that comes to mind.

More {Rest}: Lisa ends the chapter by saying that a commitment to rest is really a commitment to each other. The practice of rest builds up endurance and perseverance in your marriage. If you've just weathered a difficult time, you need rest! Even if things have been going smoothly lately, there will be more trials in the future–so build the habit of rest now! How have you rested well in the past? What would an ideal time of rest look like for you and for your husband? Dream a little bit.

Preparing For Your Next Experiment: Would you consider yourself a thoughtful person? Why or why not?

Thoughtfulness

Chapter 23

RECAP: THOUGHTFULNESS

Phylicia gifted Josh some fishing supplies during their third postpartum as a way to thank him for all of the extra work he was taking on. The gift resulted in some excellent salmon, but also made Josh feel cared about and noticed. Even though she had a lot on her own plate, Phylicia looked to his interests, too–she was thoughtful. Phylicia doesn't count "thoughtfulness" as one of her strengths, but she made this extra effort with Josh because she knew how important it was for him to feel seen by her.

"Why is it so easy to show thoughtfulness to friends, extended family, or even our kids' teachers but not to our husbands?" (From *The Flirtation Experiment*, page 139)

Do you practice thoughtfulness toward your husband? Or do you find it difficult to "squeeze him in," especially when you're thinking about the needs of so many others already?

"Do nothing out of selfish ambition or conceit, but in humility consider others as more important than yourselves. Everyone should look not to his own interests, but rather to the interests of others." (Philippians 2:3–4 CSB)

Father God, in humility, Christ considered others' needs. He considered others more important. Please help me to take that kind of attitude into my marriage and look out for my husband's interests.

MY {THOUGHTFULNESS} EXPERIMENT

Brainstorming: Phylicia notes that it can be really difficult to make allowances for your husband's hobbies, but this is a way to practice thoughtfulness. Whether it's a special snack for video game night or some extra funds for a new mountain bike, show him that you want him to enjoy himself.

My Plan: Pick ONE specific action for your {Thoughtfulness} experiment.

WHAT I'm going to do:

WHEN I'm going to do it:

Anything I need to prepare in advance:

MY {THOUGHTFULNESS} EXPERIMENT REFLECTION:

What Happened:

List a few things about your {Thoughtfulness} Experiment that . . .

Encouraged You:	*Disappointed you:*	*Surprised you:*

Our Obstacles:

His Response:

MY {THOUGHTFULNESS} EXPERIMENT WRAP-UP

To Ponder: Phylicia writes, "I tend not to see my husband as my brother. Perhaps it's a vestige of purity culture, where the guys you like are prospects and the guys you don't are 'brothers in Christ.'" Think about your husband as your "brother in Christ" for a moment. Record your reaction to that thought–do those roles match up in your head? Read Romans 12:10, and pray the Scripture over your husband, thinking of him as the "other" you are supposed to love.

More {Thoughtfulness}: Thoughtful love will help you see the successes of your husband. Take a moment to think about the ways that he is contributing to your family. List the things he has done well in the past, and the things he is doing well right now. Think about ways that you depend on the work that he does for you, no matter what that work might look like. Consider sharing the list with him–or just allow it to help form your attitude toward good regard for him.

Preparing For Your Next Experiment: Can you a recall a time when you felt comforted by God's presence? Or a time when you wanted the comfort of His presence, but you couldn't feel it?

Chapter 24

RECAP: COMFORT

Lisa and Matt walked together through the difficult season of caregiving for both of Matt's parents. Lisa knew that Matt needed to be comforted, but she wasn't sure how. As a result of decades of marriage, Lisa concluded that it wasn't always best to "play it safe" and to "give him space"–he was her husband, and he needed the care and comfort and tenderness from his wife during the season of farewells to his parents. Even though it was challenging, experiencing grief together brought Lisa and Matt closer to one another.

> **"But have you ever considered how beautifully and faithfully God comforts His people? How He desires to comfort you? He is the God of "all comfort," and He offers us His perfect comfort so that we, in turn, can comfort others. That's what his comfort of us is for—to share with others." (From *The Flirtation Experiment*, page 146)**

Where do you turn to for comfort? When life brings trials, challenges, and temptations, who or what do you turn toward for help? What about your husband?

> "Blessed be the God and Father of our Lord Jesus Christ, the Father of mercies and God of all comfort, who comforts us in all our tribulation, that we may be able to comfort those who are in any trouble, with the comfort with which we ourselves are comforted by God." (2 Corinthians 1:3–4 NKJV)

Father God, You are the Father of mercies and God of all comfort. In every difficulty, I can turn to You for comfort. Help us learn, as husband and wife, to comfort each other with Your comfort.

MY {COMFORT} EXPERIMENT

Brainstorming: Think about something difficult that your husband has been through lately–it doesn't have to be as life-altering as the death of a loved one. How could you remind him that you're there for him? Does he need an affirming note, or a loving reminder? Or does he just need your presence?

My Plan: Pick ONE specific action for your {Comfort} experiment.

WHAT I'm going to do:

WHEN I'm going to do it:

Anything I need to prepare in advance:

MY {COMFORT} EXPERIMENT REFLECTION:

What Happened:

List a few things about your {Comfort} Experiment that . . .

Encouraged You:	*Disappointed you:*	*Surprised you:*

Our Obstacles:

His Response:

MY {COMFORT} EXPERIMENT WRAP-UP

To Ponder: Early in their marriage, Lisa thought that the right thing to do when Matt was feeling sorrow was to give him space, but learning to comfort him was critical for their endurance of the trials of caregiving. How has "comfort" worked in your marriage in the past? What do your approaches to each other look like during times of disappointment or despair? Does one of you try to pull away? Does one of you feel like you have nothing to offer except possible solutions? Or do you comfort each other well?

More {Comfort}: Lisa writes, "Maybe you're asking, *But what if we are both hurting? How can I comfort someone else when I'm aching so badly myself?* I hear you. Such a situation is very difficult to walk through together—and I say this out of personal experience—but please remember that the two of you are *one.*" Have you ever been able to offer someone (it could be someone other than your husband) comfort, even though you were experiencing difficulty yourself?

Preparing For Your Next Experiment: What does it look like to have faith in someone? What words, actions, and attitudes do you say and show to a person you have faith in?

Chapter 25

RECAP: FAITH

Phylicia wanted to tell Josh that she had faith in him. This didn't feel particularly "flirtatious," but she wanted "faith" to comprise a part of the experiment. Up until this point, Phylicia's experiments had all been of her own inspiration, but totally stumped, she asked Josh. How would he show faith in another person? Josh had great answers and insight. Again, Phylicia had to deal with her own hang-ups about her actions–good ones!–being in the "fake" category just because they weren't her "own" ideas. But she realized that using Josh's input was another way to show her faith in him.

Josh told Phylicia, "It means a lot when you thank me for things. For instance, 'Thanks for doing your quiet time with the Lord,' but the difference between this and thankfulness is that faith recognizes something *I* decided to do of my own accord. Thankfulness feels more like recognizing something you wanted me to do. Which is fine; it's still meaningful. But it's different." (From *The Flirtation Experiment*, page 150)

Do you see the difference between recognizing your husband for something he decided to do and recognizing your husband for something you asked him to do? Explore that difference.

"[Love] bears all things, believes all things, hopes all things, endures all things." (1 Corinthians 13:7 NKJV)

Lord God, I want to love my husband with Your love—the love that bears all things, believes all things, hopes all things, and endures all things. Drawing on my faith in You, I want to have faith in him.

MY {FAITH} EXPERIMENT

Brainstorming: To have faith in your husband is to believe that his intentions are good, even though he isn't perfect. Start there—do you believe he has good intentions toward you? Do you believe that he's on your team? Then, go further. Offer him some recognition for a choice or action he made on his own.

My Plan: Pick ONE specific action for your {Faith} experiment.

WHAT I'm going to do:

WHEN I'm going to do it:

Anything I need to prepare in advance:

MY {FAITH} EXPERIMENT REFLECTION:

What Happened:

List a few things about your {Faith} Experiment that . . .

Encouraged You:	*Disappointed you:*	*Surprised you:*

Our Obstacles:

His Response:

MY {FAITH} EXPERIMENT WRAP-UP

To Ponder: Phylicia points out that our culture obsesses over spontaneous expressions of love. Love that asks for any ideas is considered "fake." She asks, "Are you hung up on displaying love because you fear being 'fake'? Do you think only spontaneous expressions count?" What do you think–is love more genuine if it's spontaneous? Do you expect spontaneous expressions of love from your husband?

More {Faith}: Even though "Faith" is nested in Session Five (Love Perseveres), Phylicia focuses the attribute of "faith" on "believing all things" (which would seem like it fits into Session Three–Love Trusts). The famous actions that love takes in 1 Corinthians 13 build on each other and interconnect deeply. What other experiments from the earlier sections do you think could contribute to your marriage's ability to persevere–to endure hard times with some measure of grace?

Preparing For Your Next Experiment: Do you know anyone that you would call "tenderhearted"? Who, and why?

Session Five Conclusion:

Love Perseveres

GENEROSITY, REST, THOUGHTFULNESS, COMFORT, FAITH

You want a love that perseveres and a marriage that endures trials. How can you and your husband create that kind of marriage? By being generous to other, especially with your time. By insisting that the other person gets the rest that they need. By learning how to be thoughtful in the ways that the other receives attention. By giving comfort to each other in times of sorrow. And by believing in each other–by having faith in each other–through the mistakes and mercies that make up everyday life.

Rate yourself on these scales of one to ten, one being "Never," five being "Sometimes" and ten being "Always." Go with your first instinct, not with what you think you are supposed to say.

NOTE: If this tracker isn't helpful, DON'T USE IT. This is about honest time for reflection–not condemnation or judgment of yourself.

Intentional: I take specific actions to strengthen our marriage and show him that I love him.

Never				Sometimes					Always
1	2	3	4	5	6	7	8	9	10

Faithful: I am a safe place for him. I do not mock him or call him names. He can tell me things and be confident that I won't tell everyone else.

Never				Sometimes					Always
1	2	3	4	5	6	7	8	9	10

Hopeful: I am grateful for our past and I see redemption in it, even in the difficult things. I am excited about our future together.

Never				Sometimes					Always
1	2	3	4	5	6	7	8	9	10

Joyful: We do more together than just the necessities–we create time for each other and we laugh together.

Never				Sometimes					Always
1	2	3	4	5	6	7	8	9	10

Covenantal: I am confident that, through God's grace, we will uphold our marriage covenant.

Never				Sometimes					Always
1	2	3	4	5	6	7	8	9	10

Session Six

Love Never Fails

Tenderness, Covenant,
Hope, Healing, Joy

Chapters 26 – 30

We're moving into our last session, Love Never Fails. Don't feel intimidated by that title–of course, we can all keep growing through the mistakes we will keep making in our marriages. The love that never fails isn't ours–it's God's. Marriage is a picture of God's love for us–though marriage only lasts until death, God's love will last for eternity. Through the witness of marriages built on God's love and faithfulness, we show the world that God's love always rejoices, always protects, always trusts, always hopes, and always perseveres–it is God, not us, who never fails.

These final five experiments are set up to help you look to the future and to the past–to a marriage covenant that upholds until death what you vowed to each other on your wedding day. We'll discuss the meaning of lasting tenderness, of unshakeable covenants, of steady hope, of continued healing, and irrepressible joy. Founded on the love that never fails, these experiments have the capacity to bring change (even if it's a slow change) to the experience of your marriage in the present.

Tenderness

Chapter 26

RECAP: TENDERNESS

Lisa's inspiration for this experiment came from an odd source–a country music song playing in the soundtrack of a TV show. She watched Matt react to the song and felt surprised–he was obviously moved, but he usually wasn't affected by songs in that way. The experience made her wonder–could she be more attentive to his emotional state? Was she showing him enough tenderness? She made a plan to show Matt more tenderness and take an intentionally more loving stance toward him in daily situations.

"We're too inclined, consciously or unconsciously, to dismiss these (and other) biblical admonitions when it comes to our husbands. But when Scripture gives instructions to 'one another' and 'all of you,' it doesn't exclude your marriage relationship; on the contrary, it's a good place to begin." (From *The Flirtation Experiment*, pages 156 - 157)

Who comes to mind when you think of "one another"? If you have children, you spend a lot of time attending to their needs (no matter who is where throughout the day!). Even if you don't have children, it can feel like all of the tenderness you have is better used on someone you think of as weaker or needier than your husband. Do you think of your husband as needing daily tenderness from you?

____

____

"Finally, all of you be of one mind, having compassion for one another; love as brothers, be tenderhearted, be courteous." (1 Peter 3:8 NKJV)

Heavenly Father, unify us. Give us compassion for one another, help us to love each other as brother and sister in Christ. Looking to Your example, make us tenderhearted and courteous.

MY {TENDERNESS} EXPERIMENT

Brainstorming: Lisa listened to the same song every day for a month to better understand Matt's reaction. Find a way to study your husband–what moves him? How can you show tenderness in a way that he will understand–a gentle tone, a big hug, a kind word, a slower transition between activities?

My Plan: Pick ONE specific action for your {Tenderness} experiment.

WHAT I'm going to do:

WHEN I'm going to do it:

Anything I need to prepare in advance:

MY {TENDERNESS} EXPERIMENT REFLECTION:

What Happened:

List a few things about your {Tenderness} Experiment that . . .

Encouraged You:	*Disappointed you:*	*Surprised you:*

Our Obstacles:

His Response:

MY {TENDERNESS} EXPERIMENT WRAP-UP

To Ponder: Lisa writes about her acts of tenderness, "I made a point to stop what I was doing, connect with his eyes, and listen carefully to his answer." Two aspects of tenderness are tone and timing. But it can feel like some things just can't wait–not for anything! Some perspective can help with this–the practice of tenderness building toward a lasting love, on the order of decades. Some things are worth an extra minute or two now. What obstacles do you face in giving your husband a gentle tone and flexible timing?

More {Tenderness}: Would you say that you exercise tenderness toward yourself? Is there anything that you're still hanging on to, any past mistakes or struggles for which you haven't accepted forgiveness? How do you think these things affect your marriage? Take a moment to remember God's incredible tenderness towards you. Pray Ephesians 4:32

over yourself and your marriage: "And be kind to one another, tenderhearted, forgiving one another, even as God in Christ forgave you" (NKJV).

____

____

____

____

Preparing For Your Next Experiment: How would you define the word "covenant"?

____

____

____

Covenant

Chapter 27

RECAP: COVENANT

Phylicia and Josh made it through the first difficult years of marriage clinging to their covenant–the unbreakable promise and binding agreement they both entered into on their wedding day. A few years in, they committed to weekly counseling sessions to improve their communication and understand each other better. As Phylicia puts it, the counseling was an excellent way to "tend our covenant." They celebrated the endurance of their covenant with a gifted photo shoot in Hawaii. The pictures represented an incredible gift–the gift of a covenant that would not break.

"To keep a covenant is not just to avoid infidelity but is to keep free from contempt. It means fighting for the vow that was made—not fighting *with* each other but fighting *for* each other. To battle on your knees and in your heart for the union an entire world wishes to bring down. Keeping a covenant looks a lot like war." (From *The Flirtation Experiment*, page 164)

Do you remember your wedding vows? If you have a copy, or a recording, or a video, take some time to review them. How do you fight for your husband? What kinds of practices keep your marriage free from contempt?

"After these things the word of the Lord came to Abram in a vision: 'Fear not, Abram, I am your shield; your reward shall be very great.'" (Genesis 15:1 ESV)

Lord God, You spoke these words over Abram, making a covenant with him, promising him a future that You kept at all costs. You are our shield. You keep Your covenants. You are the great reward.

MY {COVENANT} EXPERIMENT

Brainstorming: The photo shoot was a celebration of the covenant, not a necessary step toward keeping it. Celebrate your vows–scale that celebration according to your season. Read your vows to each other on a date or arrange a picnic with some friends at the place where you got married–celebrate!

My Plan: Pick ONE specific action for your {Covenant} experiment.

WHAT I'm going to do:

WHEN I'm going to do it:

Anything I need to prepare in advance:

MY {COVENANT} EXPERIMENT REFLECTION:

What Happened:

List a few things about your {Covenant} Experiment that . . .

Encouraged You:	*Disappointed you:*	*Surprised you:*

Our Obstacles:

His Response:

MY {COVENANT} EXPERIMENT WRAP-UP

To Ponder: Phylicia notes that sometimes "marriage feels like nothing more than a drawn-out argument with intermittent date nights." Think back over the years of your marriage. Have you ever felt the way that Phylicia describes here? Take the time to think about the ways that the experience of marriage has changed; look for patterns and cycles.

Can you think of specific times when you fought for your covenant? Can you think of times of peace during which you enjoyed the fruits of a covenant kept?

More {Covenant}: As you think about your covenant and ways to celebrate it throughout your marriage, instead of just on your wedding day, think about the unbreakable shield and protector that you have on your side: "In keeping the covenant, in seeking God's will for our marriage to stay strong and unified, *the covenant kept us*. Christ keeps His own." What events or struggles in your marriage can you look back on and say to yourself, "the covenant kept us?"

Preparing For Your Next Experiment: When was the last time you danced with your husband? With anyone else in your family? Be pretty generous with this one–dancing in the kitchen is dancing!

Chapter 28

RECAP: HOPE

Lisa and Matt's fifth child, Avonléa Hope, spent months in the NICU before coming home. The doctors told them that their tiny baby girl, born with severe special needs, would never walk or talk–her life would be one of limited awareness and constant medical difficulties. Twenty years later, Avonléa has defied predictions–she knows and loves her family, and she often surprises them with her insight. The whole family pours persistent hope into the life of their precious daughter and sister.

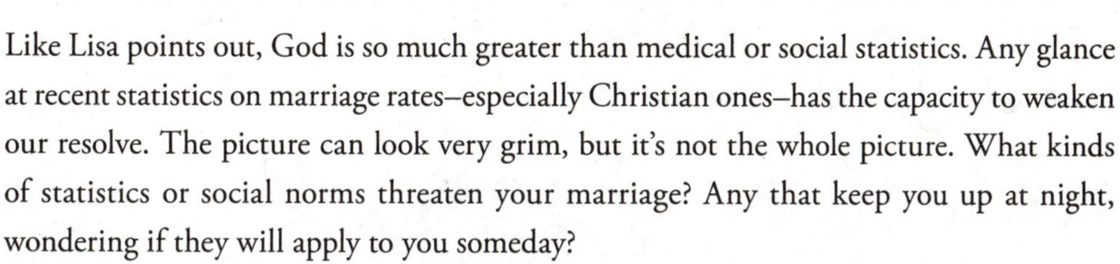
"But then my mind went back to the name God had graciously given us for her—that promising Hope—and tearfully considered how much greater He is than any medical or social statistics." (From *The Flirtation Experiment*, page 171)

Like Lisa points out, God is so much greater than medical or social statistics. Any glance at recent statistics on marriage rates–especially Christian ones–has the capacity to weaken our resolve. The picture can look very grim, but it's not the whole picture. What kinds of statistics or social norms threaten your marriage? Any that keep you up at night, wondering if they will apply to you someday?

"O Israel, hope in the Lord;
For with the Lord there is mercy,
And with Him is abundant redemption." (Psalm 130:7 NKJV)

Lord our God, with You there is abundant redemption. You always give mercy, no matter how grim or daunting the situation seems. Give us hope when everything seems hopeless.

MY {HOPE} EXPERIMENT

Brainstorming: Lisa took her family–including Avonléa–dancing. It was an expression of years of hopes fulfilled. For your marriage and your family, what looks like "dancing"–how could you express that you're choosing joy anyway? It could be as simple as a walk in a park that signifies walking on together.

My Plan: Pick ONE specific action for your {Hope} experiment.

WHAT I'm going to do:

WHEN I'm going to do it:

Anything I need to prepare in advance:

MY {HOPE} EXPERIMENT REFLECTION:

What Happened:

List a few things about your {Hope} Experiment that . . .

Encouraged You:	*Disappointed you:*	*Surprised you:*

Our Obstacles:

His Response:

MY {HOPE} EXPERIMENT WRAP-UP

To Ponder: We've visited the concept of "hope" already, with the experiments in session four. One of those experiments was about "Blessing"–speaking God's favor over a person or a situation. The statistics and stories we hear can act as anti-blessings, crowding out hope and the possibility of a good future. What words of blessing can you speak in hope over your marriage? What words of blessing do you need to hear your husband say about your marriage and your family?

More {Hope}: Lisa recommends looking up Bible verses about hope. Look up seven of these verses. Start with the ones conveniently listed in the chapter: Psalm 39:7, Psalm 130:7, Romans 15:13, Isaiah 61:3, and Ephesians 3:20. Start with a specific situation in your marriage or family that you've had feelings of hopelessness about. Spend a week praying the "verse of the day" over that situation.

Preparing For Your Next Experiment: Write a bit about a time that you experienced "healing"–physical, relational, or spiritual. What was the wound? How was it healed?

Chapter 29

RECAP: HEALING

Over the six years of their marriage, Phylicia and Josh each endured wounds inflicted by the other. Spouses hurt each other all the time. The antidote to this cycle of hurt–and the only way to heal–is to lay your marriage at the foot of the cross; to see that the wounds Jesus endured are the wounds you've received and inflicted yourself.

"Both of us have deeply wounded each other, wounds that have slowly healed to scars—but even scars twinge sometimes. In marriage, 'forgive and forget' is often impossible. I flip a page in a photo album and my stomach drops; that old pain rises. Is healing possible?" (From *The Flirtation Experiment*, page 176)

Do you think that it's impossible to "forgive and forget" in the context of marriage? Or would you challenge that thought? What does forgiveness look like in your marriage? How do you apologize to each other when you've hurt each other?

____

____

____

"But He was wounded for our transgressions,
He was bruised for our iniquities;
The chastisement for our peace was upon Him,
And by His stripes we are healed." (Isaiah 53:5 NKJV)

Father in Heaven, Jesus was bruised for our iniquities and wounded for our transgressions. By His stripes, we are healed. Bring healing into our marriage in the places we need it the most.

____

____

MY {HEALING} EXPERIMENT

Brainstorming: Maybe these experiments have helped you recognize deep hurts in your marriage. Is there a logical "next step" that you've been resisting–like counseling, or renewing your vows, or giving or receiving forgiveness that has been withheld? What would the first move be toward that "next step"?

My Plan: Pick ONE specific action for your {Healing} experiment.

WHAT I'm going to do:

WHEN I'm going to do it:

Anything I need to prepare in advance:

MY {HEALING} EXPERIMENT REFLECTION:

What Happened:

List a few things about your {Healing} Experiment that . . .

Encouraged You:	*Disappointed you:*	*Surprised you:*

Our Obstacles:

His Response:

MY {HEALING} EXPERIMENT WRAP-UP

To Ponder: It can be easy to feel like your husband's hardheartedness and sin is a constant barrage against your wholeness and happiness. It's hard to remember the truth that Phylicia asserts: "The person most deeply wounded by the sins of our husbands is not us but God." Make time to ask God for this grace: "I want to see my husband the way that You see him." Later, come back and write the ways that that prayer changed your perspective–even if it was just a little bit.

More {Healing}: Phylicia writes, "Sometimes I need to remember just how much I'm forgiven before holding a measuring stick against Josh." What helps you remember and receive God's forgiveness? Is there a particular passage of Scripture or physical place for prayer that helps you? How could you incorporate this knowledge–"by His wounds I am healed–I'm *forgiven*"–into your life?

Preparing For Your Next Experiment: How do you imagine the very last years of your marriage? Think of a hopeful version of that time and write down a few of the details.

Joy
Chapter 30

RECAP: JOY

It was almost like Lisa and Matt woke up one morning and found themselves in the "empty nester" category. They hadn't been dreading that season–Lisa often talked about how much she was looking forward to it. But they had some redefining to do–they wanted this season of their marriage to be as full of joy as their years raising children. Lisa came up with a plan to celebrate their transition together–watching a sunrise in a beautiful setting.

> "We're called to choose joy when life brings changes—even difficult trials—that we would never choose for ourselves." (From *The Flirtation Experiment*, page 183)

How do you feel about change–whether it's a big or a small one? Does the concept excite you? Or make you feel out of control? Does it bring feelings of peace or anxiety?

Think about a change that brought you joy, and write about it. Think about a change that required you to choose joy, if there was going to be any at all, and write about that.

> "For His anger is but for a moment,
> His favor is for life;
> Weeping may endure for a night,
> But joy comes in the morning." (Psalm 30:5 NKJV)

God, seasons of life will change, but You offer joy to us through everything. Please give us perspective as we move through our current season of marriage–looking to you for joy.

MY {JOY} EXPERIMENT

Brainstorming: Lisa's choice for an activity was perfect for this experiment, because it captured the change from night to day. Could you catch a sunrise or a sunset with your husband to celebrate the joy that's lasted through changes? A list of these joys would add a lot to the experience of the moment!

My Plan: Pick ONE specific action for your {Joy} experiment.

WHAT I'm going to do:

WHEN I'm going to do it:

Anything I need to prepare in advance:

MY {JOY} EXPERIMENT REFLECTION:

What Happened:

List a few things about your {Joy} Experiment that . . .

Encouraged You:	*Disappointed you:*	*Surprised you:*

Our Obstacles:

His Response:

MY {JOY} EXPERIMENT WRAP-UP

To Ponder: Lisa writes, "For the believer, joy is one of the strong characteristics of genuine Christian faith—a fruit of the Spirit (Gal. 5:22). It's what we experience in God's presence." One of the greatest threats to joy–for each of you–is missing out on God's presence.

How do you find God's presence? In silence, or in prayer together, or in God's word? What can you do to prioritize and recognize His presence in your daily lives?

More {Joy}: James writes, "Count it all joy, my brothers, when you meet trials of various kinds" (1:2, ESV). Think of something that has happened recently that you'd qualify as a trial–it doesn't have to be earthshaking. What was your reaction? Choosing joy in the midst of a trial is a way to entrust your marriage to the love that never fails. How do you think you could remind yourself to choose joy?

Session Six Conclusion:

Love Never Fails

TENDERNESS, COVENANT, HOPE, HEALING, JOY

The Flirtation Experiment is coming to a close. No matter how long this experiment took you–a matter of weeks, or months, or even a year–we hope the results will last for a lifetime.

These experiments looked forward–to a marriage covenant kept like it was promised, until death. To a marriage that ultimately points toward God's great love for the world. Build your marriage on the foundation of the love that will never fail–the love of God, the sacrifice of Christ, the presence of the Holy Spirit. And, for the sake of your marriage, never stop flirting. Never stop growing. Choose joy.

Rate yourself on these scales of one to ten, one being "Never," five being "Sometimes" and ten being "Always." Go with your first instinct, not with what you think you are supposed to say.

NOTE: If this tracker isn't helpful, DON'T USE IT. This is about honest time for reflection–not condemnation or judgment of yourself.

Intentional: I take specific actions to strengthen our marriage and show him that I love him.

Never | | | | Sometimes | | | | | Always

1	2	3	4	5	6	7	8	9	10

Faithful: I am a safe place for him. I do not mock him or call him names. He can tell me things and be confident that I won't tell everyone else.

Never | | | | Sometimes | | | | | Always

1	2	3	4	5	6	7	8	9	10

Hopeful: I am grateful for our past and I see redemption in it, even in the difficult things. I am excited about our future together.

Never | | | | Sometimes | | | | | Always

1	2	3	4	5	6	7	8	9	10

Joyful: We do more together than just the necessities–we create time for each other and we laugh together.

Never | | | | Sometimes | | | | | Always

1	2	3	4	5	6	7	8	9	10

Covenantal: I am confident that, through God's grace, we will uphold our marriage covenant.

Never | | | | Sometimes | | | | | Always

1	2	3	4	5	6	7	8	9	10

Husband Appendix

HOW TO USE THE HUSBAND APPENDIX:

You have options here. Most of the questions are written with the understanding that your husband knows the experiment is going on–if you're going for more elements of surprise, you might want to use them differently or re-write them. Feel free to hand these questions right over to him–there's space after each question for him to write a response. Or read through the questions, select the ones that work, get rid of the ones that don't, and be inspired to write a few more of your own. This appendix is a starting place. There are at least two questions for each of the experiments.

After you've decided what you're going to ask him, make a plan about when you're going to ask him. Maybe you want to tell him about the experiments and leave a sticky note in the appendix for the questions. Maybe you'd rather have these conversations face to face. If the whole feedback concept feels weird, get a little silly–email him the questions in one of those ridiculous font options and ask him to translate it and send the answers back.

No matter what you do, get some feedback from your husband! You won't know much about the results of your Flirtation Experiment unless you talk to him.

SESSION ONE: Love Rejoices

Affection

1. What do I do that makes you feel loved? Do you feel loved when I say encouraging things to you, or when I touch you without being asked to? What about when I do an errand for you that you felt stressed about?

   For more ideas, consider taking the Five Love Languages test–the five love languages in this test are "Physical Touch," "Acts of Service," "Words of Affirmation," "Receiving Gifts," and "Quality Time."

2. What did you think when I tried reaching out to touch you–was it funny, or awkward, or sweet? Are there actions that make you feel noticed that you wish I would do more often?

Passion

1. Come, my beloved,
   Let us go forth to the field;
   Let us lodge in the villages.
   Let us get up early to the vineyards;
   Let us see if the vine has budded,
   Whether the grape blossoms are open,
   And the pomegranates are in bloom.
   There I will give you my love." (Song of Solomon 7:11 – 12 NKJV)

   These are some lines from the Song of Solomon–does it sound like the man or the woman is talking to their "beloved" in these lines?

2. When I did my passion experiment, I wanted to tell you, "Come, my beloved." I know I don't do that perfectly, but I want to do it more! Was it different from our "norm" when I approached you/responded to you with passion?

Playfulness

1. I think that one of your favorite things to do is ____________. When did you start _________, and do you remember what made you love it so much?
2. I want to play with you more–I don't want to give you the pressure of judgment, and I'm willing to try something new to do this with you! We don't usually ________ ____________________ together (briefly outline your playfulness experiment).

Kindness

1. To do my kindness experiment, I thought of times during the day when I struggle the most to be kind to you. What times of the day do you think are difficult for us–for me, or you, or both of us? I thought of ____________. Can you think of others?
2. One of the authors wrote in the book, "I reasoned that if I punished him for disappointing me, then hopefully he'd try harder the next time." She was taking a very blunt look at her own attitude. Do you feel or see this kind of pressure in our marriage, coming from either one of us to the other?

Desire

1. How has the experience of desire changed for you since we've been married? This is kind of a weird question, but I'm really curious - do we have sex as often as you thought that we would? Are we having sex as much or as freely as you'd like to?
2. My experiment was all about wanting you for you. What do I do that makes you feel wanted for who you are–not just for the things I want you to do for me?

SESSION TWO: Love Protects

Adventure

1. What comes to mind when you hear the word "adventure"? What place have you always wanted to visit? What new activity have you always wanted to try? Have you always dreamed of going there or doing that, or was it inspired by something recently?
2. I suggested an adventure because I wanted to try something new with you, even if it was just breaking up the daily routine. Do you feel comfortable trying new things, or does it feel strange to you?

Laughter

1. One of the authors wrote about God being the God who laughs–and then she offered several Scripture references that backed up that attribute (Galatians 5:22–23, Psalm 16:11, John 15:11, and Zephaniah 3:17). Do you think of God this way–as the God who laughs?
2. Do you feel "responded to" when you try to make me laugh? Or do you feel like I hold back my responses from you? More broadly, do you wish that there was more laughter in our marriage?

Celebration

1. Can you remember a celebration that we had that you really enjoyed? Maybe a birthday party or a backyard cookout?
2. What's something that you've done recently that you felt very proud of? Did I notice and respond to your success in a way that made you feel recognized?

Attraction

1. How would you define the word "chemistry," in the context of how couples feel when they are together? Do you think that married couples are supposed to have chemistry?
2. My experiment involved writing down things that attracted me to you, just in day-to-day life–this is one of the things that I thought of that I find so attractive about you: ________________________________.

Connection

1. When Adam first sees Eve, this is what he says about her:

> And Adam said:
> "This *is* now bone of my bones
> And flesh of my flesh;
> She shall be called [a]Woman,
> Because she was taken out of Man." (Genesis 2:23 NKJV)

He recognizes that she completes him, that he wants to be in a relationship with her.

2. If we didn't have any other factors to consider, what activity would you want us to spend more time doing together?

SESSION THREE: Love Trusts

Vulnerability

1. Do I let you see me when I'm feeling weak? Or do you think that I try to hide my weaknesses from you?
2. Here's something that's been going on in my heart and in my head lately: ____________________ (choose a specific struggle or situation that your husband can pray for you about) Would you pray over me about this?

Mystery

1. "Three things are too wondrous for me;
four I can't understand:
the way of an eagle in the sky,
the way of a snake on a rock,
the way of a ship at sea,
and the way of a man with a young woman." (Proverbs 30:18–19 CSB)

Solomon is writing about the mystery of marriage with these lines–he's saying that, of all of these beautiful images, marriage is the most incredible of all. What elements of "mystery"–as a good thing!–do you see in marriage?

2. How has your understanding of marriage changed, now that we've been married for as long as we have? Do you feel like you understand it more or less than you did when we first got married?

Affirmation

1. Would you consider yourself a "words" person? Do you feel strengthened and encouraged by kind words, or do they make you feel awkward?
2. Even just around our house, do you notice the things that need to be done or need to be worked on, or do you tend toward noticing things that have been taken care

of or done well? What about in other places–maybe at work, or in your relationships with your family?

Refuge

1. Can you remember a time when you were small, before you were a teenager, when you felt unsafe? Or when you needed something that no one was providing for you? What was that like for you?
2. What activities or places represent "safety" to you? When do you last remember feeling "very safe"?

Friendship

1. What comes to mind when you read John 15:13–15–What do you think it means for Jesus to call his disciples friends and to lay down his life for them? How can we do the same thing for each other?
2. One interest that I thought of that we share in common is ________________. Can you think of others? When was the last time that we connected over this interest?

SESSION FOUR: Love Hopes

Delight

1. What do I do or say that signals to you "I'm glad that you're here"? What kind of attention do you like? Are there kinds of attention that make you feel uncomfortable?
2. When we meet at the end of a day, what kind of greeting do you think you're going to get? Are you ever surprised by something that I do (or don't do) or say?

Respect

1. How do you receive respect? What words or actions make you feel respected? What words or actions make you feel disrespected?
2. One of the authors writes about how showing honor to others is a primary way to respect them. What do you associate with the word "honor"? How do you show honor to other people?

Romance

1. Genesis 2 says that, in the Garden of Eden, Adam and Eve were "naked" and "not ashamed" (Genesis 2:25). What do you think that was like for them? How do you think they spent their time?
2. Do we spend our time well? What kinds of obstacles and barriers are we working against when it comes to spending time with each other?

Intimacy

1. What does it look like when I get angry? When you get angry? How would you describe the differences between the ways that you and I express anger?
2. The author writes, "I'm not a psychologist, but in my own life, anger and intimacy are connected—and according to *Psychology Today*, fear of intimacy can manifest as anger.*" Do you think that anger and intimacy are connected–do you ever feel angry when you feel like someone else is too close to one of your weaknesses?

Blessing

1. How would you define the word "blessed"? Can you remember a time that someone "blessed" you? What did that blessing look like?
2. Do you believe that God's favor is on you? Or does that not fit with your perception of yourself?

SESSION 5: Love Perseveres

Generosity

1. What's more difficult for you to give up: money or time?
2. This is supposed to be a "we're a team" question, not a "pointing fingers" question. What time allowances are we making for technology–TV shows, our phones, movies . . . ? Reading or podcasts could fit into that category, too. Is this time well allotted? Or, if we changed our habits, would we be more available to give freely of our time?

---

*Leon F. Seltzer, "Anger and Intimacy: Incompatible but Unavoidable Housemates," *Psychology Today*, June 12, 2019, https://www.psychologytoday.com/us/blog/evolution-the-self/201906/anger-and-intimacy-incompatible-unavoidable-housemates.

Rest

1. At the end of a typical week, would you say that you feel rested?
2. How could we make time for more rest in our weekly life? Do you think there's anything that we could give up for the sake of prioritizing each other?

Thoughtfulness

1. What kinds of words and actions from other people (maybe our relatives or other people you encounter day-to-day) do you regard as particularly thoughtful?
2. The author notes that you're both my husband and my brother in Christ. Would you typically think of me as your "sister in Christ"? Or is that a strange combination to you?

Comfort

1. What's the difference between "upset" and "sorrowful"? Can you think of a time you felt "upset"? What about "sorrowful"?
2. What signals "comfort" to you? When you're truly sad or hurt, do you want to talk about it? Or is presence without a lot of talking more helpful and meaningful to you?

Faith

1. Do you ever feel pressure to be spontaneous in your expressions of love for me? Like, with lots of surprises and grand gestures?
2. What does it look like to believe in each other's good intentions?

SESSION 6: Love Never Fails

Tenderness

1. Would you describe yourself as "tough" or "tender"? What word would you use to describe me?
2. Can you think of things in either of our pasts that would make us favor "tough" over "tender," or the other way around?

Covenant

1. What do you remember about the day that we got married? Is there any particular moment or sense memory that stands out in your mind?

2. Do we say "I love you" in front of other people? Why or why not? When was the last time I told you that I loved you in a place where other people could have heard us?

Hope

1. Are there any statistics you've heard about marriage or raising kids that scare you or intimidate you?
2. What is your greatest source of hope–is there a quote or a verse or a story from your past that gives you reasons to feel and be full of hope?

Healing

1. What actions, words, and attitudes convey "forgiveness" to you? What did the process of giving and receiving forgiveness look like in the family that you grew up in?
2. Where in our marriage do we need to pursue healing together?

Joy

1. What do you imagine we'll be like as a couple growing old together?
2. Can you tell me about a moment that you felt or experienced God's presence? What was that like for you?

Hopefully, you got some good feedback from your husband through these questions. Maybe you even learned something about the communication styles that both of you prefer. As you move forward into the rest of your marriage, remember that you always have options. You can always keep trying, you can always keep asking–you can always keep doing new things in the spirit of *The Flirtation Experiment*.